Eton repointed

also by J. D. R. McConnell
Eton—How It Works

The Cloister Court (1442 and 1726) as restored between 1953 and 1960: the original stone of the arches replaced by Clipsham stone; the buttresses extended to the level of the relieving arches; the stone facing of the upper storey completely replaced; the battlements, window mullions and string courses reinstated and every inch of brickwork repointed.

Eton repointed

The new structures
of an ancient foundation

J. D. R. McConnell

with photographs by
Ray Williams

Faber and Faber · London

First published in 1970
by Faber and Faber Limited
24 Russell Square London WC1
Printed in Great Britain by
W & J Mackay & Company Ltd, Chatham
All rights reserved

ISBN 0 571 09211 x

This book is dedicated
to the benefactors of Eton—
all who have enriched this school
by their munificence, their wisdom,
their craftsmanship or their toil

Acknowledgements

Any writer undertaking the task of recording what has been accomplished at Eton during the past twenty-five years could be excused for feeling a sense of inadequacy. When I embarked on it I realized that I would be greatly dependent on others for material, information and advice. Now that this book has been completed I would like to express my thanks to all who have helped me, and especially the following:

Mr Graham Watson of Curtis Brown Ltd, my literary agent, who advised on the various methods by which such a publication might be brought into being.

Mr Alan Pringle, my editor at Faber and Faber, and all the departments there who contributed to its preparation and production.

Ray Williams, whose photographs provide such an excellent portrait of Eton in 1969.

The architects who spared so much time and patience to interpret their problems to a layman: Mr Peter White-Gaze, Mr Stephen Bertram, Mr Ian Scott, Mr A. E. Duley and Lord Holford himself.

The many who put their time and memories at my disposal, among them Sir Claude Elliott, Sir Robert Birley, Mr Arthur Villiers, Mr Oliver Van Oss, Mr Rex Fripp and the Appeal Committee.

My colleagues and other members of the Eton staff who bore with my enquiries, especially the Bursar, whose precious files I so often ransacked, and Miss Lawson, who introduced me to the two million words of the Provost and Fellows agenda papers.

Miss Ireland of Hirasec, who turned my tortuous script into neat type and Mr G. C. Fawcett, who read my proofs. My wife, Meg, who helped, advised and encouraged me at every stage of the undertaking.

Penguin Books Ltd have kindly given permission to quote from Professor Nikolaus Pevsner's book, *Buckinghamshire*, and APB International (representing Methuen and Co Ltd) to quote from *Annals of Eton College* by Wasey Sterry. Mr Christopher Hussey authorized me to use a number of quotations from his book, *Eton College*, as well as his tables of masters occupying boys' houses up to 1952. The British Constructional Steelwork Association approved a quotation from Lord Holford's article in *Building with Steel*. Mr John Piper generously supplied notes on the design of windows in College Chapel.

Contents

Foreword

The Fellows of Eton asked James McConnell to write this book on the understanding that he should have free rein. So this is not an official memorandum written by a Committee and approved by the College. It is a personal account by the author of what has happened during his own time as a master at Eton and the selection of material and illustrations and the judgements on policy and performance are his alone.

The record shows, through the eyes of a witness, the changing face of Eton; changing yet abiding. It illustrates that Eton, besides being a school, is also a Foundation which must care for its buildings, its collections, its Library as well as for its scholars. It reports how a generation of men have tried, as best they knew how, to retain what excels in their heritage and yet make use of new methods and skills in preserving, in living and in teaching.

This is an unending process. What has been achieved in these years has come about through the foresight and generosity of a large number of benefactors, small and great, from the Founder to the present day. These men have been ready to back their belief in Eton by giving their time and money. This is what conviction can still do for private education. It may not persuade all those who disbelieve to alter their opinions. But only the bigoted could withhold respect for this monument of faith.

Caccia.

The Provost's Lodge,
Eton College,
Windsor, Berks.

Part One

1 · The aftermath of war

The purpose of this book is to show how an ancient foundation has been reshaping its structures to meet the requirements of the present age. During the past twenty years more building and restoration has been undertaken at Eton College than at any time since its original construction in the fifteenth century. Those of the old buildings which were of historic or artistic importance have been repaired and preserved. Where modern structures were required they have been built. Meanwhile, within that framework, a parallel change has been taking place in the academic, recreational and social life of the school; Etonians, their teachers and their governors have been readjusting methods and attitudes to a changing society. An eighteenth-century scholar who returned today would certainly feel bewildered by the changes he found on the Oppidan side of the Windsor–Slough road. But if he crossed the Long Walk and passed through the archway into School Yard his first impression would be that this group of historic buildings had remained much as he left it two hundred years ago. Closer inspection however would betray the scars and the graftings, like the face of a shell-blasted friend saved by the plastic surgeons.

The unknown German aircraft captain who shed his surplus bombs over the blacked-out Thames Valley on the night of 4th December 1940 limped home towards the Reich with little knowledge of what he had done. Some impish fate guided the two missiles on to Eton College. The first plummeted into Savile House, once the abode of a Head Master but then the residence of the Praecentor. It exploded in Dr. Ley's dining-room. Providentially the Doctor was late for dinner that night. The second plunged through the Head Master's schoolroom and, perhaps conscious of the enormity of its offence, went to earth deep below. There it remained till next day, while the Collegers were kept at a safe distance. The Provost, Lord Quickswood, is said to have poked it with his stick. This may have been too much for the bomb, which, after a decent pause, blew itself up. This incident occurred on the eve of Founders' Day and precisely punctuated the end of Eton's first five hundred years.

Casualties were limited to one of the busts in Upper School but the fabric suffered heavily. The scene, recorded shortly afterwards in a painting by Sir Gerald Kelly, shows a gaping hole in the ceiling of Upper School and the Head Master's room a shambles. The wooden panels on the walls of these rooms and on the staircase, bearing the carved names of countless Etonians, seemed to have been lost beyond recovery. Several of the bronze panels of the 1914–1918 War Memorial were destroyed. Near-by Lower School remained intact, protected by its massive walls, but minor damage was inflicted on the face of Lupton's Tower and the Chapel. More significantly the windows of the north, east and west sides of the Chapel were reduced to fragments. Though worshippers were destined to shiver for twelve long winters this Victorian glass was deemed no great loss. Certain masters with an eye for beauty and the requisite avoirdupoids may even have trodden on some of the bigger pieces, thus making sure that they would never be put back.

At that moment in the history of Britain and of Eton it required hope to look forward to the day when these historic buildings would be restored. Six, seven years were to pass, six, seven hundred Etonians were to be killed in battle before any reconstructions could be undertaken. In 1945, when it all ended and our independence as a nation had, for a generation at least, been secured, Eton's own problems were very acute. The war had not only put a stop to plans for improvement. It made nonsense of all financial calculations and provisions. When it was over the financial position of the College was alarming. The reconstruction which after six years of enforced neglect had now become urgently necessary was likely, at a conservative estimate, to cost many times more than the assets available. To begin with, the historic buildings had been standing for periods ranging from two to five hundred years. Apart from about £30,000 spent on the buildings in School Yard between 1874 and 1933 no major work of restoration had ever been undertaken. An eminent architect described them as 'hulks'; they were crumbling into decay, eroded by the ravages of weather and time, knocked about by enemy action, and enclosing within their massively strong outer casings a pest of notable potency, the death-watch beetle. Equally pressing was the problem of the boarding houses. Quite apart from any structural weakness the living conditions for boys were in many houses old-fashioned and unhygienic. The accommodation for domestic staff and the conditions in which they had to work were often lamentable. Under the prevailing circumstances it was a very real question as to whether the boys' houses could be made workable at all. These were formidable problems for a school with little in the way of funds for current expenditure, struggling to secure its independence. To look back twenty-five years from the point we have reached now is to appreciate the tremendous faith which was needed to envisage the restoration of Eton. It was exemplified by the Provost who, in the bleak winter of 1940, gave the masons at Ascot orders to prepare Clipsham stone and hold it in readiness for the repair of Upper School. He was to die before it was used but we, in 1970, can now say that our historic buildings have been put into condition to go on into the twenty-first century, that sixteen of our twenty-six boarding houses are now modernized, that the Etonian of today enjoys amenities for learning and recreation matched by few, if any other schools. Yet the entire cost was met without any of the financial burden being laid on the fee-paying parent. How Eton's well-wishers and benefactors came to her support with financial and other help and how their contributions were used is an extraordinary story. The following chapters try to pick out some of the highlights of a period unique in the history of a school.

2 · Finance

Eton is not a museum nor a national monument sustained by public funds but a school and an independent one at that. Yet her historic buildings must be regarded as a heritage not only of the College but of the nation and even western civilization. How could the school shoulder this immense and costly responsibility and at the same time take on the refurbishing of boys' houses, which, by 1945, had become an urgent need? Compensation from the War Damage Commission would do no more than establish the *status quo*. The total eventually claimed from that source was £98,000. This was a mere fraction of the expenses to be incurred in the next quarter century. Where did the rest come from?

Eton College finance The Founder showed foresight when he made provision for a current expenditure account and also a capital fund. The College was intended to be a place of pilgrimage but it was also solidly endowed with land. The saintly relics which once drew the pilgrims are no longer with us, though Eton still attracts the visitor equipped with camera or guide-book. Most of the land, despite Henry VIII's expropriation of the one hundred and eighty-five acres around St. James's, is still in the College's possession and is a source of revenue. These endowments however are primarily intended to maintain the historic buildings, religious and temporal, and to subsidize the education of the seventy King's Scholars. Here it must be emphasized that scholarship entry is open to all, selection is on merit alone and fees, which may be nil, are regulated to the parents' means. The reorganization of Eton's finances in 1935 reaffirmed the broad policy that the College's and the School's funds should be kept apart, that 'Oppidan' Eton must pay for itself.

The School, as opposed to the College,* derives its revenues from the fees. It has always been the policy to keep the fees to a minimum in order to make Eton available to as wide a range of income groups as possible. This, of course, is what creates our entry problem; more people want to come here than we have room for. The School could have procured revenue for new constructions by raising the fees and at the same time eased the pressure for places. It chose not to do so and the fees have continued to represent the bare cost of accommodation, education and recreation. Thus in 1920 they were £230 per annum and in 1945 they were still only £250. Increased costs and a drop in the worth of the pound

* The word College is often used to refer to the whole of Eton as a place of education. More specifically it may refer to the governing body or alternatively to that part of Eton appertaining to the King's Scholars.

have brought them up to £765 in 1970; a bit more than three times what they were fifty years ago. There must be few commodities whose price has increased so little. By 1969 building costs had risen to six times what they were in 1920.

If the fees were to be kept down, what other sources of funds could the College look to?

The Farrer Bequest The gloomy scene of the post-war period was lightened by one bright spot. Mr. Gaspard Farrer was an Etonian who had spent his life-time in banking and had never married. He is now remembered as Eton's greatest benefactor since the days of Henry VI and Waynflete. He died in 1945 and under the terms of his will Eton received stocks and shares to the value of £200,000. The Inland Revenue, on the other hand, benefited to the tune of £800,000 in death duties. Under the principal trusteeship of Lieut.-Col. the Hon. A. G. C. Villiers and later of Mr. A. H. Carnwath the Farrer fund prospered and grew. A dozen years were to elapse before any heavy expenditure was required from that source and they were years of the wisest stewardship. The result has been that the bequest successively met the cost of Farrer House, Villiers House, the rebuilding of Baldwin's Bec together with the restoration of the Baldwin's Shore area and finally the new Farrer Theatre. The residue is now providing for a maintenance fund.

The Pilgrim and Dulverton Trusts The Pilgrim Trust was the body which first raised the hope that Eton would not be left alone to cope with the repairs to its historic buildings. In February 1951 the Provost was informed that £21,000 had been granted for this purpose. In 1953 Lord Kilmaine reported that £20,000 had been contributed by the Dulverton Trust to the Eton Appeal Fund and earmarked for the repair of the Cloister buildings. Then in 1958 the Pilgrim Trust made a further grant of £15,000 which could be used either on the restoration of the stonework or the new roof of the Chapel.

The Eton War Memorial The memorial to the Fallen of the 1939–45 war is largely an invisible one. The fund has been used to send to Eton firstly the sons of Etonians killed in the war and secondly the sons of any Etonian in need of financial help. The visible evidence consists of the engraved bronze panels which have been placed below the 1914–18 memorial in the cloister under Upper School, and the cricket pavilion on Mesopotamia.

The Industrial Fund In 1957 this fund, which exists to advance scientific education in schools, granted Eton £30,000 towards the improvement of the Science Schools, and later added £2,000 for the purchase of equipment.

Other bequests Many bequests, the Camrose, the Thomas, the Andrews, the Busk and numerous others have helped Eton and Etonians in ways both seen and unseen. Yet these bequests were for specific purposes and still did not provide for a most pressing need—the modernization of boys' houses. Something new, something startling, something imaginative had to be done about this.

The Eton Appeal It was the pollution of the Thames which started the whole thing. Either the river was much dirtier or the instruments for measuring it were more efficient. In any case the hygienic warnings of medical experts could not be ignored. By 1950 bathing at Cuckoo Weir, that lawn-bordered, tree-shaded by-way of Sweete Themmes, was doomed; the Etonian summer was robbed of its most evocative element. As Cuckoo Weir was a cherished memory in the minds of many old boys the Provost felt that they might respond to an appeal aimed at providing something to take its place. But if an appeal was to be made to Etonians why not widen its scope and put before them the whole problem: how to meet rebuilding costs, estimated at a million pounds, without over-burdening the fee-paying parent? 'If Eton is to maintain her position and her independence, her only course is to appeal to the generosity of her supporters.' These were words written by the Provost, Sir Claude Elliott, whose vision, dedication and financial good sense steered Eton on to its course towards prosperity.

So began a movement which was to transform the financial position of the School. There is room here for only the briefest account of its development, and of the unstinted time, thought, energy and money which were contributed by so many; they made possible a great part of the improvements described in this book.

FINANCE

The Appeal was launched at a dinner given in London by Arthur Villiers, at which his guests prevailed upon him to become chairman of an executive committee. Three months later a larger body, the Etonian Committee, was formed and it included some very eminent names. It had been decided to work on as personal a basis as possible and therefore in November of 1950 the Provost invited seventeen conveners to the Lodge. These conveners, each of whom represented one of the Eton houses, were to be the spearhead of the Appeal and, working through house committees, would approach potential donors direct. By June 1951 the total subscribed amounted to a third of the target and the number of conveners meeting at 15 Lombard Street had risen to forty-three. Of the possible 10,160 donors 2,519 had responded and a decision had to be taken on 'when to fire the second barrel'.

At this point there arose the vexed question of places in the school for the sons of Etonians. One proposal was for a school entry system which would enable them to be given some priority. At a meeting with the conveners the Head Master pointed out that such a system would have a deplorable effect on houses, but he undertook that the interests of Etonians would be considered in every possible way. He advised fathers to have confidence in the General List entry system even if no definite place in a house could be offered till the last minute. During the ensuing years some hard words were written and harder ones spoken. But on the whole the assurances of Robert Birley were justified. Nearly all Etonian parents using the General List have in the end obtained places, provided that they did not abandon hope and go elsewhere and provided that their sons were up to Common Entrance standards. A survey for the year 1961 showed that all such had obtained places, and that in fact sixty per cent of the school were sons of Etonians, a far bigger figure than in any other school. In the last two years no Etonian's son passing Common Entrance at the first attempt has failed to obtain a place.

During the next few years the Appeal Fund advanced slowly. In June 1957 the first covenants were beginning to expire and conveners were invited to Eton to see for themselves what had been done. The position now was that close on half a million pounds had been given, but there was still much to be done in the way of building and improvement. So the decision was taken to establish the Appeal as a continuing fund to which all generations of Etonians would be asked to contribute. An executive committee was formed, a permanent secretary appointed and an office opened in Weston's Yard at the dark end of the passage said to be haunted by the ghost of Shelley. By 1962, thanks to the unsparing efforts of committee and conveners, the total number of donors had risen to 4,743, and by the end of 1969 the total given or promised was of the order of £800,000.

Three principal sources, the Foundation, the Farrer bequest and the Eton Appeal have therefore borne the weight of expenditure over these twenty-five years and in almost equal proportions of one-third each. Foundation money has been made available for a number of projects but up till 1970 mostly for the historic buildings, the Farrer fund has financed the special schemes mentioned above, whilst Oppidan Eton has received the lion's share of the Appeal. This is natural, for though the contribution of old Collegers to the Appeal was substantial it was former Oppidans who by weight of numbers produced most of the cash.

This surely has been bread upon the waters, for not a penny of these costs has fallen upon the fees. Nearly twenty years after the Appeal was launched it can be claimed that the confidence of those who supported it has been rewarded, whilst the fears of those who doubted have largely been allayed. The original bequest of Gaspard Farrer has been expended several times over. The endowments of the Founder have borne fruit five centuries later. Of course there have been mistakes, opportunities lost, monuments to misunderstanding erected, affronts to individual tastes perpetrated. But it would be hard to find an instance where the husbandry of funds and their use was and still is accompanied by so much reflection, so much debate and, yes, so much critical examination. The knowledge that people care so passionately is one reason why an independent place of education draws so much goodwill to itself. But there is also the conviction that here is something worth preserving, not only academic standards and ethical values but also an artistic and architectural heritage.

3 · Architecture in a total environment

There is not space to pay tribute to all those who have played their part in the rebuilding of Eton—the quantity surveyors, the contractors and consultants, the stonemasons, brickwork pointers and labourers, not to mention our own college personnel. The architects however are in a special category. No one who delves into the records of a massive programme of building such as this can fail to be impressed by the comprehensiveness and the complexity of the architect's task and the crucial role which he plays in the shaping of a society. His work is usually subject to the comments of experts on architectural style who possess an expertise to which this writer lays no claim. Such comment however is usually based on subjective observation of the completed building. An attempt has been made in this book to see some of the problems involved from the architect's point of view and to discover why certain solutions were adopted.

The critics tend to compare all works of architecture with those notable buildings where the architect, working on a *tabula rasa*, is in a position to 'make a statement'. At Eton the situation is very different. One architect compared the College to a cherished Gladstone bag whose owner wants it to be made serviceable but still look like a Gladstone bag. Where historic buildings are concerned the need is to preserve or restore what is already there. Planning boys' houses involves the resolution of conflicting forces and a blending with existing structures. Even the new theatre, as will be seen later, designed itself. There is much at Eton that is sacred. That is to say it is sacred for the time being. Take, for instance, the oriel window that looked over the Long Walk from the Corner House. It was a Victorian accretion but it was dear to the hearts of many, perhaps because Disraeli was said to have written *Coningsby* behind it. The movement of a few bricks may provoke a storm from a staff with a well-developed sense of the aesthetic and a conviction that they care as much for historic Eton as anyone.

Yet to the architect who came from an industrial or commercial project to this academic setting the change, though it involved time and discussion, was refreshing. It was stimulating to know that people noticed and cared so much about how things were done.

As the war ended the architects for the College were Seeley and Paget; it was Sir Charles Peers who advised on the decayed condition of the older buildings

Perspective aerial view of Eton by Lawrence Baker, F.R.I.B.A.

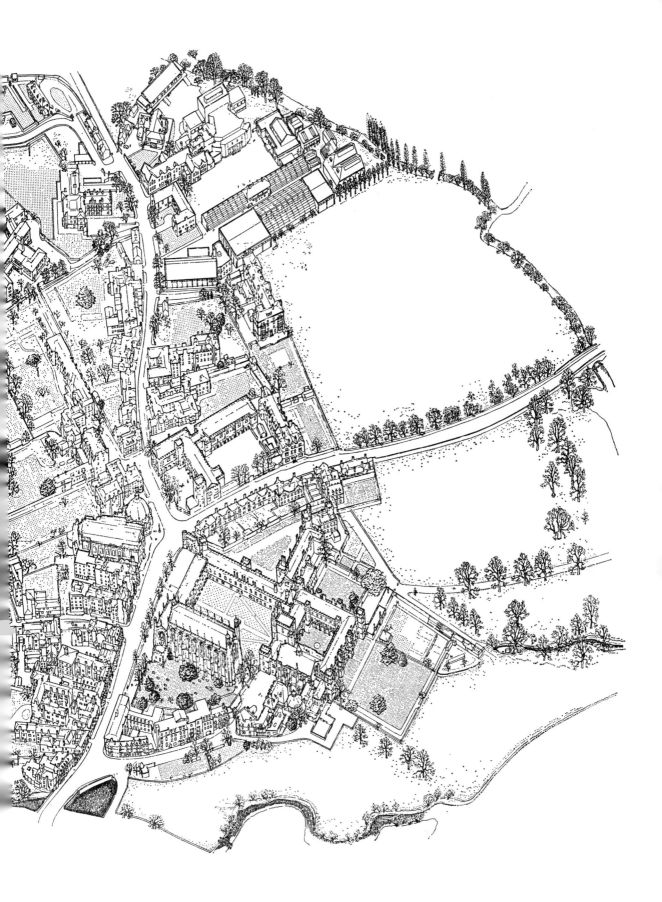

and whose firm dealt with the repairs to Upper School. In 1947 Professor
Holford was called in by the War Memorial Committee to advise them on a
visible memorial, and very soon afterwards by the Farrer Trustees to give his
views on the southern aspect of the Chapel. In 1949 he was asked by the
Provost to become consulting architect to Eton College. Thus began an
association which has continued for these twenty years. During that time
Professor Holford became Sir William and later Lord Holford. Though he has
supervised and advised, the bulk of the work has been done by Mr. E. A. Duley,
assisted by Mr. I. Scott. They have become as closely identified with the life of
Eton and as familiar with its foibles and eccentricities as anyone working here.

In 1950 no proper survey of Eton was available. The Victorians had done
nothing about this, though Eton had been a pioneer of municipal services. The
available papers were learned or sentimental and dealt with details. Holford
proposed therefore that his firm should undertake a thorough Survey of Eton.
It took longer than was anticipated. Gas mains, sewers and drains had to be
located, soils and flood levels tabulated, each house surveyed in detail, the
ownership of land and buildings verified. The resulting report with its
accompanying maps and diagnosis of every boys' house was presented to the
Provost and Fellows in July 1953. 'The College now has for the first time,'
Holford wrote, 'an accurate survey, a complete schedule of condition, and a
comprehensive background for a development policy.' In the outcome this
survey has provided and still provides the basis for the improvements that have
been made. It was always accepted that the Survey would be available to other
architects, but it was not until 1964 that Mr. Stephen Bertram was called in to
participate in the refurbishing of boys' houses. Other projects lay outside the
collegiate area and brought in different firms of architects. Mr. Michael
Pattrick designed the Andrews boat house, Mr. H. J. Stribling most of the
masters' residences, Mr. Clifford Culpin the Agar's Plough cottages, Mr. David
Hodges the swimming pool and Mr. Peter White-Gaze the new theatre.

Most building projects involve special problems but at Eton they were
particularly acute. The immutable rights protecting Lammas land restrict space.
Even when the Thames is not in flood the water table is high; in some places a
hole dug to only a few feet fills with water. The subsoil offers no firm purchase
for foundations and in recent years the noise of aircraft has presented a fresh
difficulty. But the severest hindrance of all is that the school is in action for two
hundred and fifty days of the year. Not always has it been possible to decant

whole houses and let the contractor work on an empty building. Then there are the regulations of the Ministry of Town and Country Planning to which work on scheduled buildings is subject; even the gauged mortar used for 'monumental pointing' is specified. The importance of pointing, incidentally, can be seen by comparing certain Eton buildings. College exemplifies monumental pointing at its very best. (Virtually the whole of this area is the handiwork of Mr. Bill Knight.) The Watergate building is an imitation of monumental pointing which dispenses with the need to drench the walls beforehand. Hawtrey and Durnford houses show Victorian pointing, when coal dust or the dust from iron foundries may have been mixed in the mortar.

The biggest headache of all has undoubtedly been caused by the pest dubbed *xestobium rufovillosum*. The Death Watch Beetle rates capitals in all the College documents. This insect, which makes more serious inroads than its colleague, the furniture beetle, homes unerringly on wood with the right moisture content and protein value. Oak in the Thames Valley is five-star quality and available to a satisfying extent in the timbers of our ancient buildings. The beetle has a three-year life cycle and then, about midsummer, it comes to the surface, gives up the ghost and drops down dead. If the College has provided for five hundred years a fare of good learning for poor scholars it has also furnished a habitat for numberless beetles, which here have prudently restrained that knell-like ticking which gave the species its name. It is understandable that by the mid-twentieth century the Fellows began to feel that they had done enough for *xestobium rufovillosum*, despite its Latin title.

If the Beetle was the villain of the post-war building programme Clipsham Stone has been the hero. During recent years it has come to be accepted as *the* collegiate stone. It has qualities which were lacking in its now unobtainable predecessor, Kentish Clunch. Quarried near Peterborough, it is a limestone with great durability and hardness. It can be satisfactorily cut with a diamond saw and case-hardens well when exposed to weather. Clipsham dust when mixed with a lesser proportion of white Portland cement sets in a form which is even more durable than the original stone and can be worked with equal ease. The pure stone has been extensively used on the historic buildings and the pre-cast version is to be found on many of the others. It is predicted that both will endure for another five hundred years.

Looming over every new building project has been the spectre of rising costs. Here are some figures which give an indication of what this can mean:

In 1843 two boys' houses, Hawtrey's and Durnford, were built at a cost of £5,168 each.

In 1899–1901 Waynflete and Westbury were built at a cost of £14,220 each.

In 1937 Mustians was built for about £40,000.

In 1950 the cost of a new house was estimated at £100,000.

By 1960 that estimate had gone up to £160,000, at the cheapest standard.

By 1968 the cost of major improvement to an existing house was estimated to be £100,000.

4 · The historic buildings

This book deals only with restoration or new work done since 1945. Earlier and more authoritative writers have done justice to the historic and architectural interest of Eton's buildings.[*] It is enough to record that here we have one of the most important groups of historic buildings in England, exemplifying the styles of several different periods and blending together with remarkable harmony.[†] The dates range over a period of three hundred and twenty years. The Chapel, the north side of School Yard, the Cloisters, College Hall and Kitchen were built between 1440 and 1490; Lupton's range, the east side of School Yard, in 1517–20; Upper School, the west side of School Yard, in 1670 and 1689/91; the Brewhouse and bakehouse in 1714; the Library and south arcade of the Cloisters in 1729: the upper floors of the Cloister Court in 1758/66.

The Chapel The Chapel or Church of St. Mary is the single most important building and has also been the subject of the most interesting work. Inspection in 1948 indicated that the enormously strong outer casing concealed serious deterioration and damage. In the English climate no large building, even of stone, can be left uncared for without suffering. And of course wear is worse on the bleak north side than on the south. The stonework of the Chapel was weatherbeaten and disintegrating because of stone decay, which Sir Charles Peers described as a contagious disease, comparable to cancer. It could be cured only by cutting away the infected portions. The stained glass windows had been blasted by the 1940 bomb. The East window, the largest church window in England apart from the cathedrals, had suffered eighty-five per cent damage. The tracery had survived but the upper and lower lights were beyond repair. Of the north clerestory windows all eight required remaking. The south clerestory had come off more lightly but repair would be complicated and expensive. In the ante-chapel the north window was damaged beyond repair, the others were bulging and needed repair and restoration. Unbeknownst at this time the Death Watch Beetle was at work in the wooden roof whilst damp seeping through the walls was ruining the wall paintings. About this time Christopher Hussey wrote: 'Eton Chapel resembles many other English places

[*] *The Pictorial History of Eton College.* B. J. W. Hill. *Eton Guide.* A. C. Austen Leigh and R. C. Martineau. *Eton College.* Christopher Hussey. *The Buildings of England. Buckinghamshire.* Nikolaus Pevsner.

[†] See map on p. 55.

and institutions in awaiting, battered yet serviceable, the new complexion to be given it by a new epoch, the resources of which, spiritual and material, are yet to be proved.'

The work of repair started in 1950 and has continued unremittingly since. The best way to explain what has been done is to conduct an imaginary tour and point out the features as one comes to them.

The first detail of Eton which strikes the eye as one approaches through the Home Park or drives down the new motorway is the roof of the Chapel with its soaring turrets and pinnacles. Of the twenty-three pinnacles four had been replaced in 1939–40. In 1948 many were in urgent need of repair, as were the buttresses; there was some danger from falling masonry, especially on the south side. Many of these pinnacles and the carved stonework on the tops of the buttresses have been replaced by Clipsham stone from the Peterborough quarries. All these are hand carved by such craftsmen as Mr. Jack Eastaugh; the rough shape is boasted out by the mason's assistants and the final form imparted with hammer and chisel. The wooden turrets topping the north-east and south-east corners have been rebuilt with materials which will withstand the attacks of weather and time. They are covered with a fine wire-mesh invisible from the ground. This prevents pigeons from penetrating into the Chapel, for such an incident inevitably leads to distress. The imprisoned bird starves slowly to death, and in the silent moments of services the swish of its wings suggests a dove descending. So there is a sense of outrage when it has to be shot.

At the time of the original building different stones were used to give the soaring walls a textured effect—Kentish Clunch, Heath, Bath and Huddlestone. To preserve this effect Portland, Clipsham and Wheldon stone were inserted, each of them offering a different shade of cream. The work was carried forward by trial and error, the results being noted at each stage. An awful example of how such replacement can go wrong was provided by the exterior of the ante-chapel; it had been originally of Headington stone but had been entirely resurfaced with Bath, thus losing its authenticity.

The principal entry to the Chapel is via the ante-chapel staircase. This was one of the first parts to receive attention. The Death Watch Beetle had attacked the supports of the roof beams; the tenons had disintegrated along most of their length. A completely new roof was put in, made up of materials which would thwart the attacks of pests and weather. Copper was used for the exterior. The interior concrete coffer roof was, in its day (1952), something of

an innovation, partly because it was a pre-cast construction which simply had
to be lowered into position and partly because it made use of 'exposed
aggregate'; that is to say you can see the pebbles mixed up with the khaki-
coloured concrete.

Though not exactly a treat for the eye it has indeed required no maintenance,
apart from an occasional flick with the cobweb-brush. The bats, which fled in
1952, have never returned. The staircase (seventeenth century) was at the same
time restored. Nine successive coats of paint, each consisting of several layers,
were stripped from the banisters to expose the original oak, and the treads of
the staircase replaced with two-inch oak steps on a steel carriage. It was from
under this staircase that the workmen salvaged a penny-farthing bicycle and it
remains a mystery how it came to be there.

The ante-chapel itself, which had suffered from bomb damage, was an
interesting job of restoration because it typified many of the processes used
elsewhere. Here the jambs and mullions of the windows had sheared through as
a result of vibration. They were repaired. The bulging windows were mended,
reglazed and cleaned. Miss Howson arranged the surviving parts of the north
windows against a background of white glass. Much of the stonework was
washed down and reinstated; where possible it was rubbed back to a new hard
face, otherwise it was cut back to the vertical bonds and new stone put in. The
original jambs were of Huddlestone, the mullions and tracery were of Bath.
The restorers used Clipsham, which they worked on the site. Here as elsewhere
in the Chapel soft-jointing was employed to allow for expansion and
contraction. A new lintel was cast and placed over Waynflete's door, the
Provost who in 1488 added this ante-chapel to finish off Henry VI's
uncompleted structure. The five angel corbels placed just below the springing
line of the roof are stone sculptures which were repainted during the restoration.

In the Chapel itself the dominant feature is the East window. One of the first
tasks of the College after the war was to replace the Victorian glass work with a
new window. It was the subject of very great controversy and passions ran
deep. A number of eminent artists in stained glass were considered, opinions
solicited from a great many sources. The Dean of York extolled the virtues of
the Flemish glass in King's College, Cambridge, pointing out that no window
contained less than one-third of white glass, and in some cases two-thirds. The
whole tone was 'sparkling and silvery', and 'nobody complains of a lack of
colour in that mighty series'. The Celtic style of stained glass if used at Eton

'would wage perpetual war on the architecture'. Lord Crawford, on the other hand, had journeyed to Ireland where he spent a week getting to know the work of a Miss Evie Hone. His conclusion was that her work was 'incomparably the finest modern glass that I have seen and nothing of such importance has for generations been made in this country'. His opinion carried the day and Miss Hone was towards the end of 1949 invited to submit designs. On seeing the designs the College Architects, Messrs. Seeley and Paget, asked to be allowed to dissociate themselves from the scheme of reglazing. In the words of Lord Mottistone, 'Miss Hone's designs are so wholly at variance . . . with the aims and craftsmanship of the fifteenth century that we could not conscientiously, nor with the necessary zeal, prepare the stonework for their reception.' The Provost and College were not to be deflected and on this noble note Seeley and Paget departed and William Holford and Partners took over.

Miss Hone was aged fifty-one, a Roman Catholic and Irish. Her studio was in Dublin. She was a member of the modern Celtic school, much influenced by Michael Healey (1873–1941). Her drawing, to quote the Dean of York, was 'hieratic and angular, completely non-realistic and decorative, replete with symbolism'. Her colour had the glowing deep brilliance of the twelfth and thirteenth centuries, whilst using every legitimate modern device: larger pieces of glass in variegated textures, the hardest, blackest painting of lines and folds, the use of hues rare and unknown in ancient glass—peacock blue and greens with many other unusual tones of red, blue, purple and green.

Miss Hone's grand design ingeniously combined a vertical with a horizontal concept. The lower section represented the Last Supper, the upper the Crucifixion, whilst the small openings in the tracery contained symbols of the Passion. An interesting suggestion from the Governing Body was that 'among the spectators at the Crucifixion might be included Simon of Cyrene, who was by tradition a black man . . . it would emphasise the fact that Christ is the Christ of the black as well as of the white.'

When in the course of time (1952) the scaffolding was taken down and Miss Hone's tremendous work was revealed with all its stark challenge the controversy was not ended. When asked for his opinion, Sir Kenneth Clark looked from the window to the Head Master and said 'Either you have something which is architecturally right and dead or architecturally wrong and alive.' When the experts are divided the visitor to College Chapel must judge for himself.

The College now decided to invite Miss Hone to submit designs for the two windows to north and south of the big one. She accepted, but before she could carry out the commission she died. By now Professor Holford was consulting architect to the College and his vision and comprehensive knowledge of every branch of art and architecture were available. The decision was taken to treat the Chapel in two halves. The eight windows in the nave would be glazed with *grisaille* in which would be set the Coats of Arms of the principal benefactors of Eton. These would admit light to the Chapel, the *grisaille* on the south side being slightly more tinted than on the north, to balance the light. This work was undertaken by Miss Forsythe, who embarked on her task in 1952.

The eight windows in the chancel, however, were to be of coloured glass. Mr. John Piper was the artist selected in 1958 to submit suggestions. He was not inhibited by the problem of flanking Evie Hone's work. They had been friends and had bought each other's pictures. John Piper's own comments on his work are as interesting as they are modest. Inserting modern glass in an ancient building is 'always a problem, and a responsibility; but to a large extent it did not arise here as it had been faced in the biggest possible way by Evie Hone with her east window, and it was for me only a question of making a satisfactory marriage in the N. and S. walls between Moira Forsythe's heraldic glass and Evie Hone's work. This was largely a question of colour and tone transition; the more easterly windows had to be much darker than the more westerly ones—which is convenient anyway, as the sanctuary end needs less light and perhaps richer colour. And the transition had to be undramatic.' The problems dictated by the structure of the windows 'seemed to demand by their design some kind of (i) proposition (ii) resolution. Hence the Parable and Miracle scheme . . . Robert Birley was of the greatest help and spent a long time, on many occasions, in discussion with me about possible subjects and interpretations. Most of the solutions (translations into possible visual terms that might be acceptable—especially by boys) stemmed from his ideas. His understanding of the demands was remarkable and any credit here should be entirely his.' John Piper emphasizes that the windows were really a two-man job. 'I am not a stained-glass craftsman. Patrick Reyntiens takes over my full-sized cartoons, and interprets them in glass. The technique was orthodox and traditional, as I believe it should be in a mediaeval building.'

It may be said with justice that the glazing of the Eton Chapel windows lacks the unity to be found in King's. But even if she had lived Miss Hone could probably not have undertaken more than two additional windows. By the time the nine easternmost windows were completed boys born after the war were already in College Chapel. In the interim it was necessary to exclude the elements. Besides, there was the problem of cost, and work had to be done as funds became available. The War Damage Commission could be asked to pay for repair but not for expensive new creations. The success of the windows could be gauged by the tendency of boys to raise their eyes to the mysteries of the coloured glass—the change of expression which flickered over the faces in the Crucifixion and in the Last Supper when the wind stirred the leaves of the tree (alas now felled) outside the Hone window, the crying need of the clutching hands in the feeding of the five thousand, the glowing butterfly brilliance of the sowing that brought forth a hundredfold.

The coloured windows are the first and most compelling new feature of this church and very much of our own age. (The Republic of Eire, a country always aware of creative genius, has made the East window the subject of a commemorative shilling postage stamp.) The wall paintings which have been brought to light in the nave are a startling, though perhaps not a vivid contrast.

These wall paintings in the Flemish style, executed in the late fifteenth century by an English artist named William Baker, originally filled the walls up to the base of the windows. Their purpose was probably to give the effect of an aisle and thus add grandeur to the truncated design of the Founder. They have lately come to be regarded by some experts as the most important wall paintings north of the Alps. If they were in Bruges or Ghent they would probably attract thousands of visitors. At Eton they have had a rough passage but in the last half-century have been receiving the attention they deserve. In the early sixties Mr. Geoffrey Agnew reminded the College of the unique quality of the paintings and recommended their restoration. Since 1961 Miss Pauline Plummer has been engaged on the work. Her achievement far surpasses that of Professor Tristram, whose name gave publicity to the paintings in the 1920s. The task has been an exacting one. She has had to proceed by trial and error, each step dictating the next. At the very best estimate, each square foot demands two hours' work. She has had to remove layer upon layer of disfigurement, a film-strip in reverse of the history of Eton, even of England:

A protective coating of wax varnish put on about 1950, now ingrained with grime and dust from the replacement of the roof.

(In 1840, soon after the accession of Victoria, carved oak canopies were placed above all the stalls. The upper range of paintings, depicting masculine saints, was at that date completely erased. Nothing could be done about that.)

Superimposed fluted pilasters, probably added in the seventeenth century when a classical screen was built across the nave. Associated with this was some very obstinate white lead paint.

A layer of white distemper applied by the College barber on orders from the Provost in 1560, soon after the accession of Queen Elizabeth.

Some ornamental strapwork at the east end which has revealed a damask pattern and was probably added in the time of Mary Tudor. There are also some mysterious layers of dark brown paint.

Finally comes the original painting, whose technique was unusual for murals. Oil paint was used on a thin white ground applied directly to the stone of the wall and not on to a plaster.

Miss Plummer's method is very different from the nineteenth-century idea of restoration. At first it followed the accepted modern practice in Italy, used with great effect at the Campo Santo in Pisa. Paint of the right tone was dotted in wherever specks of the original colour were revealed by the painstaking cleaning. Gradually she has invented a special technique, even used an invention of her own, an electrically heated knife to cope with the white lead paint which had set harder than the original. Little by little the original artistry has come forth, revealed like a photographic print materializing in the hypo bath. The results are excellent and in places startling, especially where the dominant *grisaille* effect is illuminated by flashes of colour: the jewelry of the women, the trappings of a steed, the stained glass in a window. The devil is a red devil. The paintings are remarkable for their sheer scope, the scale of the figures, the flowing quality of the brushwork, the bold impasto, the warm effect of the lilac half-tones. Certainly the originals are worthy, but Miss Plummer's contribution must rank as an outstanding example of the restorer's art.

It is now time to give way to the impulse to let the eye follow the bunched perpendicular columns upward—to the ceiling.

In the Buckinghamshire volume of his series on the Buildings of England Professor Nikolaus Pevsner writes rather disparagingly of the roof. 'The vault is no doubt visually satisfactory and that is perhaps all that should matter. . . . Even if one grants Sir William Holford the benefit of the doubt. . . . What should it then have been like? The critic is in the enviable position of not having to give an answer. Sir William Holford's answer, coming from this particular architect, remains puzzling.'

This, of course, is an expert on architecture in action on a time-honoured system. The critic so often is in the position of not having to give an answer. He observes and, from his great fund of experience and knowledge, comments. The big point here is that Sir William Holford is still very much alive, albeit now Lord Holford, and is able to tell us the reason why.

Some eight years after the new roof had been constructed he was to write: 'The solution devised to solve the problem of roofing Eton College Chapel is certainly not important, nor significant. It did not set out to be. This was very much an *ad hoc* problem that had been more or less troublesome since the political difficulties of King Henry—which began in 1450—first checked the momentum of his grand design for Eton. Now, in the twentieth century, a community of some fifteen hundred people—to say nothing of past members of the school who have an affection for the building which they use almost every day—greatly desire that it should henceforth be as free as possible of structural troubles. If this were done with some degree of ingenuity and elegance, they were not concerned to change the course of architectural thought in the process. It was a job which established no theories, but fought its way, like Hardy's game of chess, to a practical and effective conclusion.'

By the summer of 1956 the caretaker of College Chapel had for some time been sweeping up mysterious little pellet-like objects. One day he showed one to the Provost, who sent it to the Forest Products Research Laboratory. The answer they returned shook the College to the core; the roof timbers were infested with Death Watch Beetle.

The apex of the 1699 oak roof was seventy feet above the floor of the Chapel. It could only be reached by scaffolding. When this was erected and the experts had a close look they soon ascertained that the beetle was very well installed. The full horror of the situation gradually became apparent. When a screwdriver was inserted into the timber the wood dust might pour out continuously for five minutes. Nowhere was there a two-foot length of beam that was free from infestation. It was a wonder the roof had stayed up at all. Clearly it would have to be completely replaced.

The question was, with what? The problem of cost was a very big one but beside it arose another aesthetic one. Do you, in such circumstances, put back the kind of roof that has been there since time immemorial or do you, in so far as it lies within your power, attempt to realize the original intention of your Founder? This was the question which exercised the Provost and Fellows and indeed the whole staff of Eton whilst the Chapel was filled with scaffolding, a canopy erected over the old lead roofing and the school services removed to the hospitable but distant parish church.

The wood faction at first had the ascendant and the architects were asked to produce a scheme for repair and construction in timber. But certain disadvantages soon became apparent. That solution would be costly, slow and, worst of all, subject to the same danger of infestation. 'Why', some Fellow asked, 'should we set out to provide fodder for these insects?' There was no pest which attacked stone—at least, not yet.

The solution, planned and executed by Holford and his colleague, Mr. E. A. Duley, was brilliant, novel, ingenious and pleasing. Surprisingly it was one of the 'cheapest' jobs done at Eton in the period we are considering. The work had proceeded by stages, first the investigation, then the removal of the rotting timbers and finally the new structure. At no point was a main contractor brought in. Holford Partners' quantity surveyors (Grimwade and Ainsley) dealt with the whole thing. This cut the cost to almost half what it might have been, though it placed a big responsibility on the quantity surveyor, the clerk of works and the college works department. The scheme which the architects put before the College introduced a roof which, it was thought, bore some resemblance to what the original builder intended; a pattern of ribs and panels having the geometry of a simplified fan vault springing from the shafts separating each bay of the walls. The manner of its execution was however to be entirely modern. The new roof would consist of a framework of steel trusses. On the top would be fixed the outer skin of aluminium giving protection from the elements. From below would be suspended the new stonework.

A temporary roof, forming an umbrella over the Chapel, had been placed in position to protect the work of investigation and repair. Now, whilst the rotten and infested wood was sawed into small sections and lowered down through the ghostly Chapel, at present filled with a honeycomb of scaffolding, the new materials were made ready. First in position were the steel trusses, prepared and handled with a reverence usually accorded to hand-wrought ironwork. The bottom members, in the form of an inverted T, followed the precise curve of the pre-cast transverse stone ribs. Next, the springing stones for the first course of each fan were set on the existing columns. These were of Clipsham, the original Huddlestone and Headington being unobtainable. Thirdly the ribs and panels were fed in from above and clipped or bolted by specially made plugs to the supporting framework, with soft joints between the sections. The task was complicated by the fact that the East window was—architecturally speaking—a bastard. The arch had been put in by rule of thumb in the fifteenth century. Masons' banker marks on the inside faces showed that the stones had been cut for another window and improvised for use on the present East window. The geometry of the Chapel was not true and the architects were faced with the problem of putting a symmetrical top on an asymmetrical base.

When the ribbing and panels had all been fixed in place it was felt that something was lacking, so carved stone bosses, designed by Mr. N. G. Wykes, were placed at the eight apexes.

The outer roof had formerly been of lead, but this had disadvantages. Lead creeps in response to temperature changes. It was found that the nail holes on the north side had been elongated by three-quarters of an inch, but on the warmer south side by two inches. Lead is also very heavy and the new roof had to be light. The old lead had not been there so very long. Workmen who lifted it found a wooden board on which had been inlaid four 1870 halfpennies with the words: 'Who finds this here is a pint of beer for you.' Yes, costs have risen since then. The solution finally agreed on for the new outer covering was thick, very pure aluminium. When the umbrella was removed it 'glittered like a new kettle', but now time has weathered it down to an appearance very close to lead.

So now the Chapel has a roof which most visitors would accept as part of the ancient structure. It quickly established itself as such. When a firm of cleaners was called in to sweep away the dust and polish up the furnishings one of the workmen was overheard to remark, with a jerk of his head towards the ceiling: 'Come up lovely, hasn't it, mate? Christ, you don't get workmanship like that nowadays!' In September 1959 the boys returned after a three-year exile to their own chapel, and before long the choir had accustomed itself to the new acoustics. Then that branching roof echoed to the setting by a great Etonian composer of the Psalm, 'I was glad when they said unto me, let us go into the house of the Lord . . .'.

Windows, paintings and roof are the three most interesting things that have happened in Chapel since the second world war. There have of course been a number of other changes and innumerable repairs and improvements have been made here and there. The problems of lighting and acoustics, which have been discussed since the 1920s, are not yet finally resolved. Perhaps specially worthy of mention is the embroidery scheme whereby, thanks to the dedication of many hands, the Chapel has been embellished with brilliant book cushions, kneelers and seat cushions throughout the stalls. To these has now been added a cope, donated for the use of the chaplains on high days. It represents the tree of life and is an example of modern ecclesiastical embroidery in its most striking form. Also, the pews at the chancel end have been removed and replaced by rows of specially designed individual oak chairs, which may be moved either to leave an untrammelled space before the altar or to enclose an altar placed centrally, as now used in some services. Lupton's chapel has new pews, the altar has a new frontal, the organ has been repaired, and in many places the generosity of individual donors has added some new feature or helped to restore an old one. The present condition of the Chapel is due in a very great measure to the generous friends of Eton and the love and reverence which this building awakens in all its members.

Before leaving the Chapel it is essential to walk round it and take in the view of the southern flank. This wall must be one of the most expressive in the country for it assumes dramatic colours in varied light against different sky backgrounds. When purple-grey storm-clouds block the horizon it stands out with the apocalyptic pallor of dry bones. On a sunlit day against an azure heaven it glows with the golden tints of living flesh. There is endless variety in the texture and shade of the stones, a comforting and friendly protection in the soaring bays and buttresses. This was the spectacle which so impressed itself on Gaspard Farrer, particularly as he stood in front of the present Hodgson House, that he provided in his Will for the beautifying of this part of Eton. That is the reason why this graveyard, now laid with Cumberland turf behind its lowered wall, was one of the first places to receive attention when the war ended. Almost always deserted, it is one of those rare spots where the tempo of twentieth-century hustle seems to slow down.

School Yard In Upper School damage due to enemy action qualified for a building licence as soon as the war had ended so the western range of School Yard (1689–91) was one of the first jobs to be tackled. Repairs were started in 1948 under the direction of Sir Charles Peers of Seeley and Paget. Negotiation was as important as construction in those days and there was much litigation with the War

Damage Commission and the building licence department of the Ministry of Works. This meant that work proceeded by stages. The bomb damage had been intensified by the action of the weather and, needless to say, the Beetle was enjoying the timbers. But most of the wood bearing the carved names had been laboriously salvaged and many of the bricks saved for re-use, alongside excellent reproductions specially made at Bracknell.

When the damaged section was demolished it was possible for a few weeks to stand on the steps outside School Hall and look across at Lupton's Tower, over the site where a builder of ingenuity was using a 'dumpie' to establish the disparity in levels, and pennies and halfpennies to correct them. The walls, which had showed a tendency to spread due to the lack of proper ties, were restored and then the roof structure bearing the heavily moulded plaster ceiling was jacked up into its original position and supported on steel stools which were to be concreted into the final structure. The wood, weakened by wet and dry rot, by beetles and worms, was replaced. The roof was stripped and replaced by slates closely resembling the originals. Gradually Upper School regained its former appearance and the patiently waiting embellishments of stone-work were put in place—Portland for the blocking course, balustrade and coping, Clipsham for the columns and window surrounds.

Now, the beautifully proportioned room is used for the Third Service, where new boys worship during morning chapel until there is room for them in Lower Chapel. The free-standing cross was designed and made by Mr. Gordon Baldwin.

Across the Yard and facing Upper School is Lupton's range (1514–20); it comprises Election Hall and Penzance, flanking the tower with its imposing gateway. Some of the first post-war repairs were done here as early as 1946, when it was almost impossible to obtain a licence and labour was inadequate. Only two masons were available to effect first-aid repairs to the two-storied stone oriel windows of Election Chamber and the Queen's Room. At this time the three carved stone features in the centre of the façade were renewed. The topmost is the Royal Coat of Arms of Henry VIII, which was newly carved from Clipsham stone to a design approved by Richmond Herald. The lowest presents the Coat of Arms of Eton College, sustained by a pair of angels. The centre carving is of unique antiquarian interest and depicts the Assumption of the Blessed Virgin Mary into heaven, borne aloft by angels. It reminds us of the Founder's fidelity to this concept. All three features were newly painted.

The section of building on the south side of Lupton's Tower was completely reconstructed within its outside walls in 1966. Here were provided working space and an office for the newly appointed Keeper of the College Collections, who will also be responsible for College Library and the new picture gallery. College Library was built on the south side of the Cloister Court in the eighteenth century. It is among the richest of the small libraries of England but its ceiling and woodwork looked as if they had not been cleaned since the building was completed in 1729. The hideous cast-iron radiators installed before the first war were dust traps and made the room too hot and dry. The Victorian fireplace was unattractive and hazardous, the 1930 electric lights ugly and inefficient; moreover the structure had suffered from overloading. The task of reconditioning began in 1967 and the books, including the priceless Gutenberg Bible, were subjected to another of those *déménagements* which have so characterized their history. The intention has broadly been to follow the Ackerman print of 1816; this does not show the gallery on the north side, though the Radclyffe drawing of 1844 does. The woodwork, especially the columns, has recovered its natural colour, the cloister ceiling has been plastered over the original wood, chandeliers and soffit lights supply illumination and convector heaters warmth. There is now ample space for the showcases. Unseen behind the eighteenth-century pretence a modern structure of steel girders supports the floor and the gallery. Hard by, a room available for visiting scholars or masters with groups of pupils makes it clear that College Library is no longer a secret haunt of Fellows but a place accessible to all who are genuinely interested; whilst down below the new Muniment Room has been recognized by the Master of the Rolls, under whose authority they lie, as 'a fit repository for the college archives'.

Cloister Court   Through the archway of Lupton's Tower, whose lierne vaulted ceiling provided material for the Chapel roof controversy, lies the Cloister Court. It was originally lower, lighter and more airy, shaded by a beautifully timbered lean-to roof which sloped graciously inwards from a point somewhere below the present upper range of windows. A section of the original timbers and a carved door were recently exposed and may be seen at the north-east corner of the Cloister Corridor. The upper floors, on the north and east side, were added when the Fellows won the right to take wives (1726–9).

The stone originally used for the arches of the Cloister was Kentish Clunch. Its terribly eroded condition was partly due to the fact that it absorbed moisture which expanded when frozen. Some idea of its condition may be gained from an examination of the doorways along the wall which have been left as they were. In 1907 or thereabouts a stonemason from Ascot named Bannister had put in new Clipsham stone under an interior arch at the south-west corner. Forty-five years later it could be seen that it had stood the test of time so the young Mr. Bannister to whom the work was entrusted was confident that Clipsham should be used again. In 1953 the stonemasons tackled the complicated problem of restoration with traditional Anglo-Saxon ingenuity. 'We cut away the old decayed Clunch, leaving the centre core. The new Clipsham was cramped back in and joggled and grouted. The core was left in the centre of all the columns. The arch stones were lifted up on folding wedges; no dead shores or shoring columns. It was done piece-meal. The centering was fixed two foot three inches below the soffit of the arches. Then once the key stone was in of course the arch was held by its own weight'.

The upper portion, with its battlements and eyebrowed windows, had initially been faced with Bath stone. Its condition by 1953 was such that even the knowledgeable believed that it had been covered with plaster which was peeling away. The whole area had to be refaced with new Clipsham. At the same time the other stonework, string courses and window mullions were tidied up. The buttresses which had been emasculated during some earlier renovation were taken up to a point where they seemed to make some sense, level with the bases of the relieving arches in the brickwork, thus knitting together what is really a hotch-potch. The Cloister Court now has a new scrubbed look, but there is something forlorn about this gloomy enclosure where the tones of the school clock echo hollowly and no bird dares to venture. In the centre of the profitless lawn a pitiful tube squirts water to a height of a couple of feet. Close at hand the fabled College Pump has gone dry, its crispèd spring quenched by the shaking of the foundations along Baldwin's Shore.

Half-way up a staircase enclosed by a crumbling turret a length of twisted purple cord tactfully informs the visitor that he, or she, must quest no further. Beyond lies what was once the blue corridor, and is now a green corridor, but which the writer prefers to call the Cloister Corridor. It gives access to various notable private enclaves.

The panelling here is of the eighteenth century but behind that are the timbers of the old sloping roof, still in an astonishingly good state of repair. The Beetle did make a pass at the wood in the corridor but its attacks here lacked conviction. It did not get far among the portrait prints of great Etonian figures that covered all of the wall space. They were drastically pruned when the corridor was done over in 1966.

It would be opportune at this point in the tour to call on the Head Master and the Provost, who can both be reached from the corridor, to see what is new in their residences. The former has not always resided in the comparative isolation of the Cloister Court. Head Masters have lived in the Corner House, in Savile House, in Keate House, and before that in the corner of School Yard where the Head Master's chambers still are. When the present Magister Informator came in 1963 he too suffered transient discomfort for the sake of future ease while the north-east corner of the block was turned into something more like a family home; new rooms were created, decorations carried out, central heating carried in and the Beetle given a flea in its ear. The Provost's Lodge is something of a show-piece and provides a fitting setting for some of the college paintings. In the redecorated drawing-room (1765), with its exquisite proportions, delicate cornice and key-patterned window embrasures, the best of the leaving portraits★ by artists such as Reynolds, Lawrence and Romney have been re-hung. The panelling (1624) of the Magna Parlura has been stripped to bring back the natural oak colour and the heraldic designs painted in 1853 above the fifteenth-century fireplace have been meticulously cleaned by the expert hand of Lady Caccia. But, sign of the times, the comparatively recent window flanking the chimney has now been replaced by a door leading to a modern kitchen. Near-by Election Hall has been repainted by someone who was not afraid to use colour boldly and beyond in Election Chamber the leaving portraits of Dr. Keate's pupils are hanging in concourse.

College Kitchen College Kitchen is one of the most interesting places in Eton. To its square fifteenth-century base Provost Lupton added an octagonal lanthorn. In 1962 came its turn for modernization. While the very considerable culinary requirements of College, not to mention several banquets, were met from a tiny concrete erection at the back of the Hall, the octagonal dome was taken off and

★ It was at one time a custom for pupils of distinction to present their portrait to the Head Master.

replaced by a steel structure of the same outline. It was capped by a lantern made of imperishable modern materials, but the ball on the top is the original one. In the area underneath has been installed a kitchen comparable in its equipment to that of a first-class hotel. The old fireplace is the site of an 'ancient area', where older cooking devices are displayed. In College Kitchen may be seen examples of five developments in the history of food preparation: the original fire-dogs, the clockwork spit, the big coal-fired range, the twentieth-century gas cookers and the latest in gas-fired, electrically boosted air convector ovens. The vaulted cellars under the Hall are now a cool store with terrazza shelving, the former baking ovens are refrigerators for milk and meat and what was the larder is the crash-frozen-food depot. A mediaeval table and an old lead tank have been let into the newly plastered walls which have still not completely dried out after the drenching they received when the exterior was being monumentally pointed.

In this crisply clear, odour-free and airy setting are prepared meals for the Collegers day in and day out, and banquets for special occasions in Hall; frozen food is sent out to a dozen or so masters on five days a week and there is a system whereby in emergency a whole boys' house can be supplied with crash-frozen meals for several days. Normally of course the food sent up to Hall is freshly cooked. When ready it is loaded into a specially designed, electrically heated trolley. The trolley is taken out through the delivery hall and loaded into a lift. The lift takes it up to Hall level. It is taken into Hall and there plugged in again. The lapse of time is so small that individual cheese soufflés reach the table before they drop. And when the Collegers depart, smacking their lips, the dirty dishes are consigned to the most modern of sculleries, where they are burnished by a Staines Kitchen Equipment Rotary Brush Dishwasher.

College In 1967 the King's Scholars plus their attendant staff were decanted into Hodgson House so that their premises could be given a top overhaul. Not a great deal needed to be done to New Buildings, that northward jutting wing, erected by Provost Hodgson in 1844–6. The building dividing Weston's Yard and School Yard (1440–50) was by contrast badly in need of renovation and modernization. Built between 1440 and 1450, it was the first building in Britain of any importance since Roman times to be constructed of bricks; they were made at the royal brickworks in Slough. It need hardly be said that the timbers were seriously eroded. Washing facilities were inadequate and the open stalls allotted to the more junior Collegers were not altogether satisfactory. It had been decided to deal the *coup de grâce* to Long Chamber.

The annals of Long Chamber may be read in the many volumes about bygone Eton. Suffice it to say that up till 1844 this immense room, 172 feet long, 27 feet wide and 15 feet high, provided quarters for the bulk of the scholars, who were locked into it from 6.30 p.m. till the following morning. The compassionate Provost Hodgson took the first bite out of Long Chamber, converting two-thirds of it into individual rooms. Some thirty years later the remaining space was divided up by wooden partitions into separate stalls with open tops. It was to remain thus for close on a hundred years.

In 1967 the whole of the interior was stripped out and for a short while the magnificent proportions of this enormous room with its mullioned windows were again revealed. Into this shell the new accommodation was inserted. Steel girders spanning the building raised the level of the whole floor some four or five feet to bring the windows down to a reasonable level. The central corridor with its new panelling, its low ceiling and its huge inset lights may remind one of the lower deck of a transatlantic liner, but an atmosphere of antiquity is given to the rooms by the original windows, some of which offer evocative views across School Yard to the Chapel or onto the freshly turfed lawn of Weston's Yard. There is considerable variation in the size of rooms, from the relatively spacious apartment of a Sixth Former to the ninety square-foot hideout of a new Colleger. Common to all are two new features, the stainless steel wash-basin with its hot and cold running water, and the centrally heated radiator. The built-in wardrobe-cum-cupboard is a 1967 fitting, but the old-style 'burry' has been retained as a writing desk and chest of drawers. Amid the slightly jarring modernity of swing doors and virgin panelling some eccentricities have been retained; one small room at the top of a flight of stairs has no space for a wash-basin so its occupant descends to perform his ablutions on a small landing half-way up. In the loggia, from which a flight of steps now leads down to the Master in College's door, the old table constructed of the wood from ancient beds does something to establish that this is still 'College'.

New Buildings have been redecorated and refurbished but not greatly altered. There are two new wash rooms—or 'absolution rooms', to use the term favoured by the workmen. New kettle rooms have been provided and the rooms where junior Collegers take tea have been refurnished (with money from College Trust). The College butler's room is now a boy's room and the former has a flat built out into the back yard. The Reading Room remains as it was except for the marbled chess table won by Eton in ITV's Sixth Form Challenge.

The Master-in-College's house is vast, contrary to popular belief, and there has been plenty of room to create a human and homely private side. Here again floor levels have been raised to place the windows at an acceptable height. The study has been brought downstairs and the old study is now a drawing-room. In the modernized bedroom suite stands the famed bed of the Ladies of Llangollen, now the property of the present incumbent. Much ingenuity has gone into giving the Matron-in-College more space; her bathroom is in what was once a spiral staircase and her office, with its steel cupboards, key-boards and clip-boards, occupies a room once used by a Provost for his hour of private prayer.

On the exterior of the fifteenth-century building the old leaded gutters and roofing have been removed, new timbers fitted, and a roof covering of aluminium has been placed over the whole. The masonry has been given the usual face lift; chimney stacks have been made sound, crenellations and battlements reinstated, parapets rebuilt, moulded copings scrubbed down and the brickwork overall has been raked out and repointed. Naturally, this had to be monumental pointing, carefully specified in the Estimate.

'Mortar for pointing is to be gauged mortar $\frac{1}{2}$ part Portland Cement, 1 part Lime, 2 parts fine washed Thames Sharp sand ($\frac{1}{16}$" sieve), 1 part washed sand (first pass through $\frac{1}{4}$" sieve then use residue that is left in $\frac{1}{8}$" sieve).

'Well hose over wall and tuck mix into well raked out joints, avoiding surplus on face of brickwork. Dab out face of joint with a well wetted paint brush to remove small and *leave large stones on face of joint.*

'Each time the brush is used on joint to remove surplus it must be flicked off brush, and the brush dipped in clean water before re-applying.

'Lightly hose off face of work after initial setting to remove any other surplus and whiteness on bricks.'

Brewhouse   In 1922 Christopher Hussey wrote 'Brewhouse Yard lying at the east end of Chapel is given over to silence, pigeons and choristers, which latter have now their school in the dim recesses of that eighteenth-century building whence the yard is named.' He did not find it necessary to alter that wording much when he revised his work for republication in 1952. It was still 'one of the quietest spots in Eton'.

It has not been quiet lately. The temporary concrete monstrosity that housed a kitchen for College, contractors' huts, a works department dump and the paraphernalia of heating engineers and builders have violated its peace. In 1966 the choristers had to vacate the building and move out to temporary quarters, a commercially produced standard prefabricated structure on the edge of Fellows' Eyot. They were destined never to return. The Choir sang its last in July 1968. Its going was marked by one of the most moving occasions of recent times when at the very end of the summer half the choirs of New College, King's College, Winchester College and Eton College assembled to sing Evensong in Henry VI's church. The service opened with the Founder's Prayer set to music by Henry Ley. The fortissimo passages of 'Zadok the Priest' set the echoes racing along the lofty vaults. But the final anthem closed 'pianissimo'. It was Standford's 'For lo I raise up . . .'.

'The vision is yet for the appointed time, and it hasteth toward the end and shall not lie: though it tarry, wait for it because it will surely come. For the earth shall be filled with the glory of the knowledge of God, as the waters cover the sea.

'But the Lord is in his holy temple: let all the earth keep silence before him.'

The small professional choir has gone, replaced by a larger body of boys whose homespun tone textures are enhanced by a light interweaving of more mature voices. To counterbalance the loss of the Choir School the College will in future award choral scholarships to Oppidan Houses and when the full quota has been taken up there will be fifteen such scholars at Eton.

The Brewhouse (1714) now becomes a gallery where a selection of the best pictures in the possession of the College can be fittingly displayed. They number altogether three hundred or more and have been valued at not far short of a million pounds. The leaving portraits have been well displayed in the Lodge, in Election Chamber and in certain other places such as the dining room of Baldwin's Bec. The portraits of famous Etonians from Henry VI to the present day have by tradition adorned the walls of the Cloister Corridor. The Newcastle collection of topographical and portrait prints has been displayed in Montagu James and Alington Schools. There are also the Harcourt and Hambledon collections of prints and drawings, the Swire collection of English mezzotints and the Storer print collection of French and English portraits, all of which have been displayed. But the Pilkington collection has up till now been glimpsed only fleetingly in the Head Master's chambers, whereas it is the most important collection of English water colours made since the war. The Farrer collection, which has a close affinity with the purport of this book, has hardly seen the light of day at all. It consists of outstanding examples of prints, drawings and pictures by contemporary artists recording the changing face of Eton since 1955. Robin Darwin's series of the Thames and Cuckoo Weir has hung in the schoolroom at Farrer House since 1960. Some forty others have collected in the storeroom till the moment should come for them to be displayed. Each artist has shown an interest in some particular aspect: Rupert Shephard in the new houses and the paraphernalia of construction, Sidney Worth in winter scenes, Reynolds Stone in trees and in the area round Baldwin's Bec, where he was born.

The new Eton Gallery is the brain-child of Mr. Geoffrey Agnew. There are five rooms for variable displays of the Eton collections, equipped with moveable ceiling lights which will allow flexibility of arrangement. The Gallery will also provide a suitable setting for exhibitions from outside sources. Now at last the College has the means to display as befits them such works of art as may be loaned or donated. In the ground floor room the fenestration has been restored to its original form, whilst on the first floor a barrel vaulted ceiling ingeniously disguises the steel girders which had to be put in to strengthen the building. On the top floor, reached either by the old choir-school stairs or a new spiral staircase, the eighteenth century roof timbering has been left exposed. When the Gallery was opened on November 23rd 1969 the staircase and the upper rooms were hung with the best works from the various Eton collections, especially the Pilkington. But the ground floor contained reminders of remoter times—the huge map of Venice (1611), left to Eton by Sir Henry Wotton, ambassador to that republic, paintings of Royal visits, relics of a colourful and vanished ceremony, the procession *ad Montem*.

And this may serve as a reminder to one who gazes over the new oil storage tank in Brewhouse Yard, past the flank of College Chapel to the quiet graveyard and the bustling road beyond, that we stand on ground which has patiently endured the tread of centuries. The Montem procession may be recorded in prints and memoirs but so much that was once a part of Eton life has disappeared and left no trace. Yet still the buildings remain. This house, now an art gallery, was not long ago a choir school and before that a bakehouse and brewhouse where they made an audit ale worthy of a prince's table. Now it has been restored, strengthened, made ready to go forward into another century. And in that future century, if ever it comes, what will they know about these two decades now ended, and what will they say about our present stewardship of this Lancastrian, Tudor and Stuart inheritance?

5 · Baldwin's Shore

The only boys' boarding house remaining on the same side of the main road as College is Baldwin's Bec. It forms part of that group of buildings to the south of the graveyard which came under so much discussion because of the Farrer bequest. In 1945 there was another boys' house in this area, the Corner House, as well as two bachelor colonies, Baldwin's Shore and Baldwin's End. Bekynton was a private residence attached to the Corner House. These houses formed a crescent. They turned their faces southward and their back-sides towards the graveyard. Gaspard Farrer was not the first to be offended by the buildings along Baldwin's Shore. It is said that Queen Victoria objected to the unlovely, four-storied, yellow brick block of Baldwin's Bec, which obscured the royal view of the chapel from Windsor Castle Terrace. In 1918 the architect, Herbert Baker, found it a great eyesore to Eton and an affront to the Chapel. He envisaged its eventual demolition. By 1945 the churchyard, once the site of the Church of St. Mary's, had become an untidy wilderness of tombstones, long grass and refuse concealed behind a high wall.

The object of the Farrer trust was, broadly speaking, 'to improve the buildings of Eton College the gardens and grounds belonging thereto and the churchyard adjoining the chapel by repair renovation demolition building and rebuilding . . . within the scope of a charitable trust'. In November 1945, shortly before his death, the Settlor expressed a wish that any such scheme would result in opening out the view of Chapel from the south side. It was in June 1949 that the trustees invited Professor Holford, who was already advising on the War Memorial, to express his views. He was apprised of the Settlor's wishes, but expressed his conviction that the domestic character of the crescent of buildings enhanced the view of the chapel by acting as a foil to it. Wholesale clearance would destroy that effect of intimacy. He was in favour of retaining the southward aspects, cleaning up and improving the north or churchyard side and putting the interiors into a sound state of repair.

The question arose as to whether the existing buildings really did provide the right kind of intimacy. Baldwin's Shore, a gabled, timber-framed, plastered house, was probably one of the oldest in Eton and the last surviving example of a style common in the old village but condemned during the reconstructions of the nineteenth and early twentieth centuries. Its height was modest, its architectural impact restrained. The Corner House was a pleasant red brick house built as a private speculation in the seventeenth century. Its original clean lines had been sacrificed to expediency when it was split into two

BALDWIN'S SHORE

Dames' houses, then linked to form one boys' house and a portion hived off as a private residence, Bekynton. Walls and roofs had been pushed upwards and outwards, forming an ugly barrier to the eye. But the interior possessed a quixotic charm; and three prime ministers had lived there as boys. The sanctity of the oriel window has already been noted. As for Baldwin's Bec, it provided further proof of the statement that in Eton certain things are sacred—at least for a generation. The wistaria and the magnolia on the south side had endeared themselves and the companionable windows, or fenestration, had acquired nostalgic associations.

Not for a decade was the rebuilding of the Baldwin's Shore area put into effect. By now the new Farrer House was ready and Villiers was well on the way. There was elbow room to decant the occupants of the Corner House and Baldwin's Bec and to accommodate elsewhere the masters in Bekynton and Baldwin's Shore. The general idea of the rebuilders was firstly to preserve the familiar domestic atmosphere of the southern frontages, secondly to provide on the other side a pleasing complement to the Chapel and graveyard, thirdly to create through-ways which would lead pedestrians naturally into the graveyard and present them with rewarding views of the Chapel. It goes without saying that the buildings would be put into a good state of repair and would require the minimum maintenance in future years.

The solution of the Corner House involved a change of purpose rather than style. It was to provide a number of flats for married and single masters. The outer casing was completely reconstructed with new bricks, whose crisp freshness will take perhaps a hundred years to weather, and surmounted by a tiled roof with dormer windows. The façade of Baldwin's Shore was retained, or rather put back exactly as it was. Before demolition the whole front of the building was surveyed and when it was rebuilt every window, every bulge and idiosyncrasy of the ancient walls was reproduced. The chimney stacks now rested on concrete bases, for the executive-style suites which the bachelors found waiting for them boasted no open fireplaces. The important difference however was that a passage now led through to the churchyard at the back, and a lane or alleyway curved round to the service areas of Baldwin's Shore and the Corner House. This small area repays study for it shows how attention to detail can enhance an unpromising scene. Admittedly Holford's conception of a break in the buildings which would afford a brief glimpse of the whole sweep of the Chapel buttresses was not realized. But this former slum area is pleasantly intimate, domestic and clean. Refuse bins are concealed by curving brickwork walls, the courtyard has been pulled together by the continuation of the string-courses round the buildings and their expression has been brightened by the full wooden sash window-frames in the copper roof.

If one can find three people who claim credit for putting the curve into Farrer House it is hard to find anyone who takes responsibility for what was done with Baldwin's Bec. This project has left unhappy memories with the architect. Here the necessity for compromise, the fear of novelty have resulted in an anachronism. The awful spectre of Nancy with her cleaver lurks behind the whole edifice. Nancy had been left in charge of the premises that holiday time when the architect of the Farrer trustees, with his rolled-up plans under his arm, made so bold as to knock upon the service door. It opened to reveal an apocalyptic figure, steeped in red blood to the elbows and wielding a meat cleaver. No surveys were carried out that day. The incident was an omen. For the façade of Baldwin's Bec was declared inviolate. Fearful of the consequences if an architect were permitted to 'make a statement' in this sacrosanct area the College decided to retain the existing façade with its familiar fenestration, its wistaria and its magnolia. So, while the wafer-thin front wall was supported on scaffolding, a new building was constructed behind it. This entailed enormous complications, for the fenestration dictated all the interior levels. The result is rather bogus. Apart from ten foot of wall shaved off the top the front looks the same. The rear is pleasingly collegiate, done in Clipsham stone with matching buff bricks and a copper-plated Mansard roof with wood-sashed dormer windows. But the concessions made to preserving the nineteenth-century frontage and creating a pleasing foil for the Chapel have led to certain anomalies within the house itself.

The boys' lavatories on the ground floor are fitted with clear glass and offer the passer-by an unexpectedly intimate view of Eton life. The tall, horizontal, frosted glass window above them continues below the level of the bathroom behind it. The red brick wing at the back is at a different level from the rest of the house so that tea trollies cannot circulate freely. The number of boys on each floor—eighteen on the top, fourteen on the bottom—make it hard to divide work equally between boys' maids. The dining-room being below the level of the graveyard is dark and further oppressed by its low ceiling. All the smallest boys' rooms are in one area so that the new boys to whom they are inevitably allotted tend to become separated from house life. The staff quarters, instead of providing small suites where married couples could make a home, offer rooms so small that when a double bed is put in there is barely room for the *señor* and his *señora*. The private side contains a hundred and fifty-nine yards of stairs and corridors, all of which need carpeting, but no garage was provided for the house master's car. The boys' rooms on the third floor have unguarded windows, but the drawing-room on the first floor has been fitted with guard rails to prevent the occupants from falling out. However, central heating, a modern kitchen, wood panelling and parquet floors do much to make these imperfections seem bearable.

Seen from Luxmoore's garden the surviving façade now has the smug look, tempered with remorse, of an elder sister who has just got her way in a family argument and is thoroughly ashamed at having done so. It is a horrible reminder that some compromises leave no one satisfied.

The old pupil room of Baldwin's Bec is no longer there. In that space is a kind of proscenium arch in depth. Walk through it, ascend the curved range of steps to the churchyard and you will receive the dramatic impact of the Chapel, towering triumphant over all. Has the rebuilding provided it with the foil it demands? Has the wish of Gaspard Farrer been honoured?

An early print from the viewpoint of the castle terrace depicts an uncluttered chapel with its emphatically perpendicular buttresses shafting upwards from ground level. It looks stark and naked. Even in the famed Canaletto painting the church appears humpy and isolated without its attendant houses. This kind of building was never intended to hog the space all around it like today's tower blocks. Arising from amidst surrounding roofs and gables it has a kindly eminence. Notice how often the artist is impelled to present it in such a way, with pinnacles and turrets lording it above surrounding trees and temporal structures. Chapel is best seen from some way off, from the Home Park, the Playing Fields or even the new motorway. In his 1922 edition of *Eton College* Christopher Hussey, who had gazed at the Chapel from his boy's room in the Corner House, wrote: 'Out of a water-meadow it rises, somehow embodying in stone the familiar graces of the river bank. The Chapel is the epitome in limestone of the wide beauty of the Thames, of its union of grandeur with intimacy and of the picturesque with simplicity.'

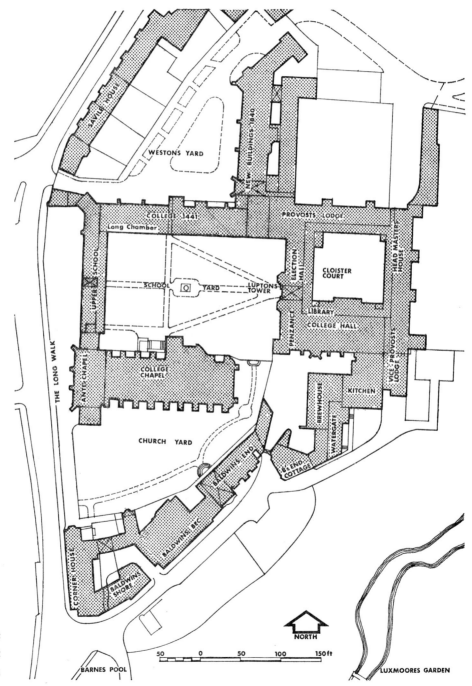

SAVILE HOUSE

WESTONS YARD

NEW BUILDINGS 1840

COLLEGE 1441

Long Chamber

PROVOSTS LODGE

UPPER SCHOOL

SCHOOL YARD

LUPTONS TOWER

ELECTION HALL

PENZANCE

CLOISTER COURT

HEAD MASTERS HOUSE

LIBRARY

COLLEGE HALL

ANTE CHAPEL

COLLEGE CHAPEL

VICE PROVOSTS LODGE

KITCHEN

CHURCH YARD

BREWHOUSE

WATERGATE

B. END COTTAGE

BALDWINS END

THE LONG WALK

BALDWINS B.C.

CORNER HOUSE

BALDWINS SHORE

NORTH

50   0   50   100   150 ft

BARNES POOL

LUXMOORES GARDEN

The
historic
buildings

(*previous page*)
King Henry VI, Founder of Eton College

Eton from Windsor Castle

School Yard in 1969, with Lupton's gateway and Tower

College Chapel from Luxmoore's Garden

From St. Mary's Churchyard

From across the Thames

A detail of repaired stonework on the Chapel

Doorway to the stairs leading to Upper School and the Chapel

Interior of College Chapel,
showing the East window and the new fan-vaulted roof

The restorer at work on the fifteenth-century wall paintings

From Lupton's Chapel, showing the sixteenth-century fan-vaulting
against the fans of the new roof

The north-west corner of School Yard from the Chapel roof.
The lighter coloured brickwork indicates the rebuilt section

The Long Walk. On the left is the eighteenth-century front of
School Yard, with the Ante-Chapel beyond

The oriel window of the Master-in-College's house

East side of the Cloisters. The stonework to the left has been repaired;
that to the right has not

The Cloisters, showing brickwork repointed and stonework reinstated

The Provost's drawing room, showing fourteen of the thirty-three leaving portraits hung there. On the extreme right are the Hon. Charles Pelham by John Hoppner (*above*) and William Henry Lambton by George Romney (*below*). On the wall at the centre are George Norbrone Vincent by Benjamin West (*above right*), The Hon. Henry Howard by Allan Ramsay (*below right*), Henry Fetherstonhaugh by Benjamin West (*above left*), William Young by Benjamin West (*below left*). The portrait in the centre is of Charles Manners, Marquess of Granby, by Thomas Gainsborough; that on the extreme left is of William Baker by Sir Joshua Reynolds

The Magna Parlura in the Provost's Lodge.
The portrait of the Founder is anonymous

A fifteenth-century door and original timbers of the Cloisters lean-to roof, revealed in the restoration of the Cloister Corridor

The College buildings from across the Thames. The house of the
Head Master is in the part to the right, that of the Vice-Provost to the left

Savile House, completely rebuilt after bomb damage in 1940

The main entrance to School Yard. Through the archway may be seen the statue of the Founder and the gateway and oriel window of Lupton's Tower. The first floor windows are those of Upper School, now double-glazed to exclude traffic noise

College Kitchen.
Some of the ancient cooking devices
can be seen to the left

Modern brickwork with simulated monumental pointing.
The new Luxmoore House and Watergate building, with
the reconstructed lanthorn and roof of College Kitchen beyond

The Corner House and Baldwin's Shore as reconstructed

Looking down on the same area from the east end of the Chapel roof

Baldwin's Bec. The Victorian façade leaning on the modern construction.
The tower contains a lift

Seen from Baldwin's End, the south-east corner of Chapel.
The tower contains a stairway

The Chapel reflected in the modern steel-framed windows of Baldwin's
Bec boys' dining room. Seen through a glass darkly are their table-ware
and trophies

The south side of Chapel and the Churchyard,
seen from the through-way under Baldwin's Bec

Farrer House. The private side

The curved south-west face of the boys' side

The boys' dining room. On the far wall can be seen the portrait of
Mr. Gaspard Farrer

Farrer House, showing the brick cornice, the brick headers and the use of
slate panels between the windows

Villiers House. The colonnade beneath the boys' wing

The south-west aspect. In the centre below is the dining room
and above is the apartment of the Dame

The extension to Penn House, showing the window of the new Library

Private Business in a domestic setting. The new garden room at Penn House

Waynflete House undergoing major restoration

Godolphin House

Lino laying

Condemned

Approved

Saw-tooth brickwork and hand-carved Clipsham stone

Durnford House. The new extension, showing decorative brickwork

New science buildings. On the left is lower chapel, in the centre the tower containing the staircase, and on the right the chemistry laboratories

In the new
science schools

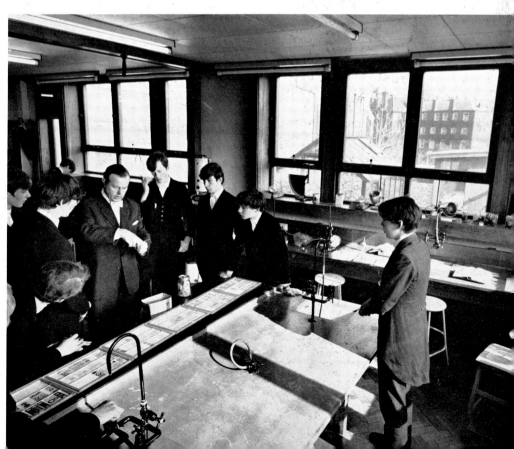

A sixth former's room in the reconstructed Long Chamber

The new concert hall in the music schools

The Farrer Hall

1 The entrance front, showing the sinuous line effect of the
bush-hammered concrete

2 In the control room

3 The workshop

4 The auditorium

5 The sliding panel is here drawn back, showing the movable rows of seats at the front

6 The sliding panel is closed and the lift is fully raised, forming an apron to the stage

Re-roofed
fives courts

Squash courts

The Andrews
boat house

The swimming pool

Interior of Andrews boat house

Pavilion on Mesopotamia, in memory of the Fallen 1939–1945

Manor House 'in the pipe-line'

(*overleaf*)

'Out of a water meadow it rises, somehow
embodying in stone the familiar graces of the river bank . . .'

Mr. Bill Knight, craftsman brick-layer and pointer

Part Two

6 · Farrer and Villiers Houses

The two Farrer bequest houses, and Villiers in particular, are probably the finest boys' boarding houses in Britain. They possess frontages which would command admiration if they were placed on a visually advantageous site but which in the confined spaces of Eton are difficult to see. Gaspard Farrer died in 1945. In 1949 a Building Committee was set up to consider among other things the new house and its site, for which Warre Park was ultimately chosen. By 1953 the position with regard to building licences was becoming easier and Sir William Holford was invited to present his plans to a meeting of the Provost and Fellows. The governing body was reticent. Holford noted: 'Everyone would be prepared to say what he did *not* like but not what he did like . . . it was left to the architect to produce "something simple and domestic but with character".' Soon the architects found themselves at the crux of a double tug-of-war. The Farrer trustees, who were supplying the funds, wanted the best materials so as to save the College future maintenance costs. The Bursar was anxious to keep costs down so that not too extravagant a standard would be set for other houses. If the governing body was reticent the House Masters' Committee did not want for ideas or words to express them. A formidable mass of detailed suggestions was offered, along with some taboos.

The basic requirements were for fifty boys' rooms on three floors, with separate areas for the private side, the domestic staff and the catering arrangements. The architects' plan took the form of an H with one stroke longer than the other. The long stroke would contain the boys' rooms, all of which would face southward, away from the garden and the rest of the building. Amidst the plethora of comment which the original design provoked two ideas stand out: one was that the whole of the boys' side should be slid a little northward, the other that the strokes of the H should curve away from each other. These curves would increase costs but would make the interior less institutional and add grace and light to the exterior. It is hard to ascribe credit for this excellent idea. The writer talked to three different people who claimed the curves as their own.

In 1956 work began on the site. The bill of quantity describes the project: 'the building is of reinforced concrete construction mainly precast with cavity wall cladding and precast floors with insitu concrete filling. The main roofs are pitched with steel roof trusses and copper roof coverings. The basement and air-raid shelter is of insitu reinforced concrete construction.' The decision to provide a deep shelter under the house and to site a heating station there is now seen as a mistake. It also led to delay at an early stage, for the deep foundations had to be sealed off and pumped dry before building could proceed. The adoption of the curves precluded building in stone. Concrete would not produce a pleasing effect because of its tendency to weather badly. The choice was for bricks, three-inch Flemish garden wall bricks which look well when new and weather down over a hundred years to a more and more pleasing hue. They were laid with a gauged mortar consisting of four parts clean sand from the Rumfold pit, two parts of Sharp Thorp or Wraysbury aggregate, one part of hydrated lime and one part of Portland cement. The joints were half-inch 'slightly raked with a rounded tool and stippled with a one-inch paint-brush to expose the larger aggregate'. The window surrounds, wall cappings and other stone dressings were of pre-cast Peterborough stone. Copper was selected for the roof because of lightness and durability, but one very authoritative opinion objected to the green colour to which it weathers. The roofs were therefore treated with linseed oil which produced a dirty brown colour. It will probably wear off within a generation. The contractor omitted to treat the whole roof, which now has a bright green section. It stands out like a leprous though exotic bald patch.

When the house was completed there were criticisms, of course; the boys' rooms were all too much the same size, the squat square chimney was more suitable to a laundry, the north wall of the boys' wing was prison-like, the whole place was on too lavish a scale. All these were limited views, for the building was a resolution of conflicting interests. It was a machine for living in. There had to be a fusion between aesthetic creativeness on the one hand and manageable maintenance on the other. The vital thing was that the house should be easily run by its occupants and flexible in use. It was not long however before all concerned had an opportunity to put into effect the lessons learned in the construction of Farrer House. No sooner was it completed than the trustees informed the Head Master that they were in a position to pay for another house. The site chosen was again Warre Park, a little further to the north; its name, Villiers, reminds us of the debt the school owes to Gaspard Farrer's friend and his first trustee.

If Farrer was made the butt of criticisms it is only fair to approach Villiers in a more appreciative frame of mind and look at a few of its considerable merits. So far from being boring or repetitive this building has a number of facets; from each of four angles of approach it presents a different aspect. The boys' block faces south and is again slightly curved as if drawing the sun to itself. Visually it rests effortlessly on an arcade of curved pre-cast stone lintels poised on brick columns. The surface of the wall takes life and texture from the restrained pattern of slightly protruding bricks. Three imaginative courses of bricks, one of them the familiar saw-tooth pattern, edge the top of the wall, forming what is in effect a brick cornice. The solid base of this block tapers very slightly inwards for the first fifteen feet or so. Unfortunately a wooden fence obscures the arcade and thus the poised effect is completely lost. The approach to the private side is between two brick walls which curve outward like arms to enclose the patio in front of a door and balcony which repeats on a smaller scale the east gallery. The design of this elevation is again slightly curved but restrained. As over the whole building, it is the details that count—the lines and curves of the low-pitched roof meeting and crossing in a mobile pattern as you walk past, the fine strip of lighter mortar that runs round the whole private block two feet below the eaves, the headers which protrude in the faintest of designs to break a plain surface, the soldier courses and saw-tooth patterns giving interest to such an unpromising feature as the tower. It is a matter of record that for these sophisticated patterns the bricklayers worked from drawings prepared by the architects showing each individual brick. Villiers House is in fact something unique in the present day: living accommodation built to optimum standards, where an attempt has been made to meet every requirement of the user within a visually attractive structure.

7 · Improvement of boarding houses

In 1949 a Building Committee was set up by the Provost and Fellows on the Head Master's recommendation. The latter was acutely conscious of the need to modernize houses and make them workable under present-day conditions. 'A sixty-five year old cook', one House Master had written, 'objects to climbing four floors through boys in order to reach a bathroom when she has finished work.' Scullery conditions in one house were so disgraceful that the domestic staff had to work till late in the afternoon in order to dispose of the debris left by the boys' dinner. Some boys' houses had only one lavatory on each floor. The committee's first report was made in February 1950, and one of its features was the proposal, in the interests of economy, to increase the numbers in each boys' house by the addition of rooms, and ultimately to counterbalance this by the suppression of a complete house. Twenty years later, as the modernization programme approaches completion, the fact is being faced that you can't liquidate a house just like that, and therefore Eton's numbers may well rise to 1,280.

The first building licences did not come through till February 1953. During that time the Holford Survey was being prepared. When presented in July 1953 it contained, among other appraisals, a detailed and systematic analysis of the state of every house with recommendations for improvement. Though not precisely adhered to, this has been the basis for all the work done since and by agreement with William Holford and Partners has been available also to other firms of architects. Some work was done on the Timbralls in 1953 and a new kitchen was put into Durnford in 1954, but it was not until 1955 that the plan really got under way with the alterations to Holland and Godolphin. Then followed a second bite at the Timbralls, and from 1956 to 1963 the two new houses were a-building. At this stage the whole question of costs came up and a reappraisal of the programme was made in the light of ten years' experience. The Farrer trustees had always preferred to accept the cost of first class materials at the building stage in order to reduce maintenance costs later. Donors to the Appeal quite naturally wanted to be assured that their money was not only invested wisely but spent wisely. It was not enough that economy was practised. Like justice it had to be *seen* that it was practised. For a school Bursary, through which was being channelled a building programme on the scale of a small town's, this was not easy. Building costs were rising with alarming speed.

'Every tender', the Bursar wrote in 1963, 'confirms one's worst fears'. In
addition builders seemed unable to complete jobs on time; this was serious
in an institution rigidly bound by the dates for beginning and ending of the
holidays. Certain tasks, such as the installation of a new kitchen, had to be done
during the summer holidays when the contractor could be given six weeks.
This inevitably raised costs since trades had to be concentrated in the kitchen
instead of being diverted to it when freed from other jobs. Overtime and week-
end working had to be accepted; and a delay in the delivery of materials could
wreck a carefully timed plan. This was one reason why the cost was five or six
thousand pounds higher when improvements were attempted without
decanting the occupants.

The high standards of the Farrer bequest houses had rather unfairly put a
label of extravagance on the College and on its architects. Some of the facts of
life, though known to those involved in the costing, were not appreciated by
outside critics. For instance, that the use of low maintenance materials costs
more now but saves money later, that a structure based on a steel skeleton and
concrete sub-floors avoids the risk of beetle and dry rot, that a copper roof and
aluminium windows should give years of trouble-free life, that the cost of
reconditioning old buildings was rising faster than the cost of erecting new ones.
There was also a burning question: what was the future of catering in the
school? If money were spent on bringing house kitchens up to standard
(since 1960 the health authorities had had the power to inspect) would it be
wasted if the system broke down and central feeding were introduced?

In these circumstances a number of very thorough investigations were made.
One of them dealt with catering. The committee formed to consider this
question became probably as expert on the subject as any in Britain. They
visited schools which had introduced central catering, such as Wellington,
Brighton and Marlborough; they had consultations with the London County
Council and the adviser to the Ministry of Health on catering and dietetics;
they even travelled to Hamburg where under the watchful eye of the Matron-
in-College they concentrated their attention on Eppendorf University Hospital
and Harburg Hospital, both known for their pioneering systems. Their
report, running to twenty foolscap pages, examined three possible alternatives
to the present system—central cooking and a central dining hall, a central
kitchen delivering hot food and a central kitchen delivering frozen food. Apart
from a number of practical objections, there was no readily available site in

Eton where a central dining hall could be built. The most promising alternative was considered to be offered by new techniques of 'crash-freezing' food cooked in automatic ovens for subsequent distribution and re-heating. But as the techniques were not fully developed it would be unwise to hurry into the purchase of experimental equipment. A pilot scheme was launched whereby College Kitchen became a frozen food depot whence meals could be despatched to houses in crises where a rescue operation was needed. Lately, this system has come under fresh examination for it has been found that a diet of only frozen food can lead in some people to an inability to eat anything at all. So meanwhile the houses continue, with greater or less travail, to operate under their independent systems.

The problem of building standards was also examined, and since Durnford House was due for refurbishing it was made the guinea-pig. The architects and their quantity surveyors co-operated with the Bursar in this. Two or three examples will show the intractability of the problems. One criticism of the new houses was that the rooms were too much the same size. But the way to economize in building is to use 'modules' or repetitive structural patterns. So to reproduce the quaint inconsistencies of the old Eton houses would be costly. The size of boys' rooms became a crucial factor; 95 square feet was regarded as a minimum and 100 as a norm, and the total square footage of building would determine the cost. For the windows the architect recommended standard metal casements for the twenty rooms of the new extension; to put in the cheapest wooden frames would have saved about £50, whilst to supply the best type of aluminium frames would have added on £1,680. The cheapest standard of decoration on the three boys' corridors would have cost £190. Half-height panelling with standard pre-fabricated hardwood panels would cost £725, but there would be no need for painting—or re-painting.

No aspersions were being cast on the products of any of these firms when the labels Rolls, Rover and Ford were applied to the three possible standards. The College decided to plump for Rover in their coming assault on boys' houses. They impressed on their architect the need to study economy and at the same time decided to engage a second firm of architects to deal with improvements to boys' houses. It was felt that this would have several advantages; it would mean that another architect would become *au fait* with Eton's peculiar problems, it would prevent the present architect from having more to do than he could reasonably be expected to handle, it would lead to a reduction in costs and would offer the possibility of making comparisons. The hope about costs has not altogether been realized but anyone who is interested enough to walk around Eton and use his eyes can make some very interesting comparisons.

So the occupants of Durnford were decanted and the extension and improvements were undertaken. The original estimate had risen from £28,000 to £35,000 and then to £78,000. But the final bill proved that even the time you spend discussing costs is costly. It came to approximately £100,000. It is amusing to recall that in 1900 the College estimated that £25 annually should be enough to cover 'interior and structural repairs' to a boys' house.

Now came the turn of Walpole, Mustians, Westbury, South Lawn, Penn, Cotton Hall and Waynflete. Certain features were common policy in all these cases. Central heating was installed, linking the house to one of the heating stations cunningly concealed around Oppidan Eton in the group heating system. Accommodation for boys was increased to bring numbers up to forty-nine or fifty. Better and more wash rooms and lavatories were put in. The whole question of furniture in boys' rooms was looked into and rationalized to make the maximum use of space; fitted wardrobes, book-shelves and cupboards have for instance been specially designed for Waynflete. The quarters offered to domestic staff were greatly improved with abundant 'toilet' amenities. Private sides were brought up to modern standards of maintenance and independence, equipped with their own 'kitchenettes' in recognition of the fact that most of today's house masters are family men whose wives do a lot of the cooking in term time and probably all of it during the holidays.

During this period Oppidan Eton began to look like a town that had suffered a bomb attack. Huddles of contractors' huts, emergency parks for workmen's cars, festoons of scaffolding, chirping transistor sets, discarded packages of sandwiches, all proclaimed the British builder at work. Amidst it all the educational system struggled on. The experiences of some of the houses which had to live through major improvements without decanting would form a bibliography on its own ranging from farce to tragedy in the proper sense of the word. Some notable exercises in human relations were carried out and tolerance became a major virtue. Often the men employed on the job were the same age as the older boys in the house and there was mutual interest in a different way of life. The personality and resilience of the house master and his wife were a vital factor whilst under some contractors the men behaved better than others. One house master arranged football matches between boys and builders, another took his coat off and showed that he was an expert carpenter himself, and wives discovered that it was necessary somehow to produce a smile of welcome when the plumber arrived at the most inconvenient moment possible. The worst problem was noise; it is hard to educate the young when a near-by saw is shrieking through metal. If the cost of rebuilding was a problem of the governing body the experience of having his house set upon by working men was a nightmare to any house master who had to endure it; the already exacting task of running a house became a labour of Hercules. So, where Eton is concerned, the word benefactor can be taken in a wide sense.

By the beginning of 1969 the situation with regard to boys' houses was that three completely new ones had been built, as a result of the Farrer bequest. Thirteen more had undergone major improvements, thanks almost entirely to the Appeal Fund. College had been reconditioned at the expense of the Foundation. Nine oppidan houses remained to be done. Now the watershed had been crossed; it was the minority of houses which had to cope with the antiquated conditions left over from pre-war years. Once again the question arose: where could funds be found to complete the programme? For the Head Master had made an important declaration to the Provost and Fellows. The independent schools would prosper and survive only if they maintained the highest academic and educational standards and this depended on the quality of teaching staff. Salary and pension rates must therefore be such as to attract and keep the best men even if this meant that the building programme had to slow down. Since then the salary and pension conditions have been improved, but at the time of writing the College are also preparing to undertake major improvements to Manor and Keate houses.

In the Appendix will be found a list of boys' houses with a brief note of their present condition.

8 · Buildings for teaching and recreation

Teaching   The expansion in numbers, reforms to the curriculum and new teaching methods have demanded more schoolroom space and new facilities. In 1969 there were 564 boys doing sixth form work and in June of the same year about 800 taking G.C.E. at various levels. The three new boys' houses each contain a schoolroom for the house master and there is also one in Waynflete. The Savile Press has been converted to Caxton Schools with eight rooms. Seven schoolrooms have been released for non-scientific teaching by the extension of the Science Schools. But owing to an expansion of the staff this still leaves a serious shortage of schoolrooms; thirteen per cent of the non-scientific staff have no room of their own and have to be peripatetic. The situation will get worse before it gets better for Keate's Lane 1 and 2 are threatened by the extension of Keate House, and Warre Schools by the plans for Angelo's. Plans to rebuild or extend New Schools have been found impracticable, though of its twenty-nine rooms fifteen of the most archaic have been refurnished, reorientated, redecorated and literally brought up to modern standards (by raising the floor a couple of feet to bring the windows down and push the master up). Two rooms in Warre Schools have been equipped as language laboratories using the Shipton Tutor system and each providing twenty-four desks. It goes without saying that teaching aids of all sorts too numerous to mention are to be found in rooms all over Eton, whilst it has been policy gradually to replace the old benches with modern desks or seats and tables. More notable has been the provision of two new examination rooms, for School Hall and Upper School could no longer cater for all G.C.E. candidates under the strict conditions laid down by the board. Placed at the top of the new science block they are spacious, well lit and scientifically ventilated.

The only important building for teaching purposes since the 1930s has been the Science Schools. In 1957 the Industrial Fund for the Advancement of Scientific Education in Schools offered Eton a grant of £30,000 for this object, plus £2,000 for equipment. The Foundation put up the rest of the money and the rebuilding was undertaken in three phases from 1957 to 1963. When it was completed Eton could claim to have as good science accommodation and equipment as any school in Britain. The implications of this will be discussed in a later chapter. One does not think of laboratories as being aesthetically pleasing but the architect, Mr. E. A. Duley, took great trouble to make the new structures worthy of their setting. The chemistry and biology block had to harmonize with Lower Chapel, Queen's Schools and South Lawn. A virtue was made of necessity and now the grass-lawned court is separated from the car park by the tower enclosing the stairs and lift. It is of brick and tapers slightly from base to summit. The surface at the top is broken by insets of soldier courses of bricks laid in a chevron or saw-tooth pattern; the roof line is edged with a slim layer of white pre-cast stone. In the block on the western side the brick used was chosen to blend with South Lawn; once again saw-tooth patterns have been used to avoid monotony and counterbalance the flat effect of the abundant window surfaces. Across the road the windows of the top floor of the physics block are sloped backwards to prevent them overlooking South Lawn with too much dominance. These may not be buildings of great beauty but close examination shows how thought has been given to embellishing their utility.

The Music Schools on the same side as the physics block are the work of another architect, Mr. Stephen Bertram. When these were rebuilt there was need for additional space to encompass more practice and teaching rooms, three rehearsal rooms and a larger concert hall. Yet the site was bounded on the one side by the public road and footpath and on the other by inviolate Lammas land. The solution was to raise the concert hall to the second floor and push it out laterally on cantilevers. From outside the result looks functionally competent. The interior presents an uncommonly pleasing aspect. The crisp rows of green tip-up seats contrast with the natural colour of the well-grained wood of walls, ceiling and platform. Ample windows, which can be shaded by Venetian blinds, offer agreeable views of Lower Chapel to one side and green fields to the other . The four large ventilators in the ceiling assist the acoustic properties of the hall, which are excellent; the fitting of absorbent material to the undersides of the seats means that the resonance is the same when it is empty as when it is full. This is a two-way hall for it provides a rehearsal room for the chorus of the Eton College Musical Society as well as a setting for instrumental competitions, visiting performers and the delightful concerts given by the Music Circle.

Recreation When bathing at Cuckoo Weir was stopped the decision was taken to build a new outdoor pool which would recapture some of the lost enchantment. The site chosen was the northern end of Mesopotamia and, as has been seen, the cost was to be met by appealing for funds.

The idea of a pool of the normal rectangular shape was rejected in favour of a shape originally drawn on the back of an envelope by Mr. Oliver Van Oss, consisting of two oval pools linked by a channel. In 1955 the moving of earth began and once again the spectre of the water table rose from the ooze. When the concrete basin was inserted would it sink into the mud or float on a rising water table and break its back? In the end more earth was carried onto the site than off it and so far the pool has neither sunk nor floated. Earth banks were heaped up round it, lawns laid out, long-term trees planted in the brick-hard clay. All has been well, apart from the brevity and inclemency of the English summer, now restricted to a few happy days between the end of May and the beginning of July.

There are not many such pools. It is big enough to be available to the whole school without staggering the times of admission. The smaller, shallower pool is open to lower boys, the bigger, deeper end to the rest. For competition purposes a hundred-metre course with lanes can be set out using the length of the channel and the deep end. Of course it is now argued that too much money was spent on the pool and that in any case it would have been better to provide a heated indoor pool for use all the year round. The answer perhaps depends on whether, where memories are concerned, you want quality or quantity. The best way to decide might be to watch boys bathing in heated, chlorine-scented indoor baths and then compare that with the spectacle at the Eton pool on a sunny afternoon or a warm, still evening when the sun has set.

Not only have the waters of the Thames become polluted, its surface is also much more crowded. By the late 1950s it had become almost impossible to organize races on the reaches immediately upstream from Eton. So when Mr. G. M. Andrews left a bequest of £10,000 to Eton to be used as the College thought best it was decided to build a new boat house above 'locks' and a little way upstream from Boveney Church. The Andrews boat house snuggles unobtrusively into the fields that lie beside the river, modest but pleasing in its visual impact, simply functional in its purpose. The architect was Mr. Michael Pattrick. His building is a pavilion whose roofing rests on bowstring trusses of laminated timber moored to reinforced concrete outcrops springing from the concrete raft on which the structure rests. The side walls, which bear no load, are of cedar boarding joined to the roof by metal mesh. The roof is weather-proofed by dark green mineral-surfaced felt. The light and airy building is greatly enhanced when its spacious interior is filled with the slim, curved, gleaming shapes of riggers, whiffs and fours.

The touch of the same architect may be detected in the new cricket pavilion on Mesopotamia. The flat, felted timber roof rests on laminated beams supported by two reinforced concrete frames on independent foundations. The interior is stark but the visually open space between the roof and the non-load-bearing walls gives the white little building an appearance of competence blended with fantasy that is altogether suitable for the cricketing scene.

Reconstruction of the cricket pavilion on Agar's Plough, the construction of a dozen new squash courts to the south of the Field, the roofing of the fives courts with glass, the opening of a new studio in the drawing schools are some of the ways in which new building has improved the amenities for recreation. But the feature dwarfing all others is the Farrer Theatre, which makes as important a contribution to teaching as to recreation. It has also aroused more interest and controversy than any other building.

For the Farrer trustees 29th November 1965 was a crucial date. The twenty-year period would end then and any residual monies unless earmarked for a specific purpose would revert to the National Fund. The trustees determined to give Eton something that was unlikely to be provided from any other source, something that would in fact be a luxury. The original idea of a theatre, suggested by the tremendous growth of drama in the school, was changed to a scheme for a multi-purpose hall. Not only would this be more likely to qualify for a licence from the Authority; it was also more in keeping with current feelings on the use of funds. A committee of masters chaired by Mr. John Meynell was appointed to make recommendations. They visited existing theatres at Nottingham, Guildford, Coventry, Camberley, Twickenham, Ealing, awarding them marks for the features most desired. But it was Alanbrooke Hall at the Staff College, Camberley, which got top score. The firm who had built it, A. M. Gear and Associates, were selected and their architect, Mr. Peter White-Gaze, set to work on the plans. The Taylor Woodrow tender was accepted and on 5th June 1966 work began on the north side of the parade ground. When in October 1968 the new theatre was completed it was acclaimed by Eton residents with a certain reserve; which was a pity, because it is a remarkable edifice which can be appreciated only if the full story of its conception and creation is known. It is also an interesting example of what architecture and building involved in the 1960s.

The brief which the College gave the architects was detailed and complex. It provided the following estimate of usage frequencies on a mark-scale of 0–10. Drama: 10. Cinema: 10. TV: 8. Concerts: 6. Speeches: 4. Opera: 2. Revue: 2. The main spaces required included a workshop, a rehearsal room, dressing and make-up rooms, control room and projection suite. The stage had to offer flexibility in use, for conflicting factions in the School demanded proscenium, peninsular and apron stages. As it was envisaged that the hall would be in frequent use, with house plays following each other in quick succession, a fly-tower was needed where scenery could be 'flown' when not in use. This is what makes it such a dominant building, and the haystack lantern required by fire regulations adds further to the height. The seating require-ment was 400, and the shape of the auditorium was generated from the relationship of seats derived from comfort, sight lines, fire precautions and acoustics. An inexorable mathematical progression increased the final figure to 401.

When the architect remarked that the new theatre had designed itself he meant of course that certain audio-visual-geological factors dominated the planning. It is more than a truism to state that the theatre, a place where happenings must be audible, was placed 'twixt earth and sky. The earth had to be considered first. Ground level was 65.34 feet above the Newlyn Datum, which for architectural purposes means sea level. Trial holes showed that the water level is struck at 5.25 feet. The top soil is 'made ground'. At 2.23 feet sandy brown clay was reached, at 5.25 feet brown sand, at 7 feet brown gravel and sand, at 27.5 feet weathered chalk. A somewhat soggy story for the first twenty-seven feet. This was what dictated the use of piled foundations. The sky in this part of the world is noisy, to say the least. In the future jumbo jets are likely to be steered directly over Eton. The noise survey which was carried out at an early stage showed that with the wind in a certain direction civil jet aircraft heading NW passed overhead at the rate of six to seven an hour—and that was winter traffic. The report of the Acoustical Investigation and Research Organization recommended a concrete construction, since what excludes noise is mass and weight. So a very heavy building had to be placed on an infirm subsoil.

Sheer mass was needed to exclude noise but due to the high cost of piled foundations it was necessary to make the weight as little as possible. So around the auditorium, stage and fly-tower was placed an envelope of 'in-situ'★ reinforced concrete with an inner leaf of brickwork. These walls supported steel beams which carried the roof, a six-inch thick layer of reinforced concrete with an outer envelope of woodwork slabs. In parts of the building not needing such good sound insulation brick or concrete was used in whatever way was most economical.

Given these stringent necessities what could be done to make the building acceptable to the eye? Some critics have asked, why not brick? Brick was never a serious contender. Bricks cannot be satisfactorily set on piled foundations and, besides, a fly-tower with square corners would have looked even more massive. There was already enough brick in the parade ground, and School Yard proved that one building of lighter material can provide relief. Architect, quantity surveyor and contractor agreed that one must build in the materials of the age and the material of this age is in-situ concrete, unpoetic though it may sound. This particular building arouses interest because of the method used to make concrete look more attractive. Reinforced concrete contains an 'aggregate', that is an admixture of graded pebbles, sand and other materials. This is certainly not the first instance where the aggregate has been exposed; it has been a practice for thirty years. But the explicitness of the instructions given in the preambles to the bill of quantity is probably without precedent. The composition of the concrete and the gauge of the aggregate were, as is usual, specified in detail. The wooden 'formwork' into which it was poured was ribbed to give a corrugated surface, the ribs being aligned from bottom to top. When the concrete had set and the formwork was removed the whole exterior was bush-hammered with a Kango hammer, once in an upward and once in a downward direction. The ribs were also given a hand-tooled finish with a four-pound club hammer. 'Each arris', the preamble directed, 'is to be struck at approximately twelve inches vertical centres, the striking points on the two arrises of one rib being staggered. The club hammer is to be used at an angle of approximately 45 degrees to the face of the wall and the tooling is to produce a sinuous line effect to the face of the ribs.' The walls and columns of the foyer provide another imaginative use of formwork, for here the carpenter was directed to provide strongly grained planks which have left the impression of their living surfaces on the hardened concrete.

★ Mixed on the site.

The exterior of the theatre is secondary to its interior. The aspect of the building is intended not to distract attention from what goes on in it, but the auditorium is impressive with its luxurious grey seating, brick side walls and adigbo wood panelling. The ceiling, of pine tongue-and-groove boarding, is profiled to accommodate the stage lighting and stereophonic sound equipment. Panelled portions of the side walls can be slid back to give that encirclement which is desired when the thrust stage is used. Its components can be brought up from the spacious basement on an electric lift platform which can also be used as an apron stage or an orchestra pit. Though the end-stage layout has priority, there is no frame to the proscenium opening, the height of which is variable between fifteen and seventeen feet. Out of sight beyond are the dressing rooms, the rehearsal room and the workshop, an important feature since it is intended that as far as possible boys themselves should prepare and produce dramatic performances. Just how much of a stimulus this can be was shown by a remarkable 'College' production of Anouilh's *Becket* in Lent 1969.

If the appearance of the theatre makes one forget that it has other purposes besides drama a walk through the projection suite shows how versatile it is. The control room houses the stage lighting console and other controls for sound, auditorium lights, fire-alarm and communications. There is also a tape-deck and gramophone turn-table. The projection room contains equipment of a high standard including two Eidophor 35 mm. projectors teamed with a cinema screen big enough to take Cinemascope; 16 mm. auxiliary attachments enable them to show smaller gauge films as well. There is equipment for reproducing stereophonic or non-aural sound through screen and auditorium ceiling speakers, as well as two slide projectors and one overhead projector. At a later stage, if funds are available, two further features may be added; they are videotape equipment for recording TV programmes for later projection onto the cinema screen and electronically assisted resonance to increase the reverberation time of the hall when it is used for orchestral concerts. Even without these refinements Eton possesses in this new gift of the Farrer Trust an amenity which has not only high entertainment value but offers infinite scope for educational purposes. It marks the final phase of what has been a monumental benefaction and provides a fitting point at which to conclude this account of the building done at Eton in the past twenty-five years.

Inevitably the account is incomplete, for still more rebuilding projects are in the pipe-line; besides the continuing work on boys' houses there are the restoration of College Hall, plans for a new Sanatorium and Mathematics Schools, the creation of a common dining-room for masters, and so on. Perhaps most interesting is the reorganization of School Library, which contains a surprising number of rare books. The present plan however embodies the purchase of books to make the collections more up to date and comprehensive, whilst structural and administrative changes will make the Library more accessible and attractive to boys of all ages.

9 · Academic changes

If there have been changes in the architectural appearance of Eton there have been even greater changes within its walls. Eton has always been changing, sometimes because of its own sense of the need for new attitudes, often to keep in line with what is happening in the wider field of education. Developments during the past twenty years or so have completely altered the ethos of the School and made the Etonian of today someone quite different from the earlier generations. Changes are far too numerous to be dealt with fully in this final section of the book. There is only space to outline briefly what seems most significant and to make a quick reference to minor novelties.

Curriculum Not for some years after the war did Eton stir from the leisurely, gentlemanly attitude towards education which allowed the true scholar to explore the heights, while the less academically minded took things more easily. Those were the days of the Grand July examination, when the scripts of Eton's scholars were looked over by dons at Oxford and Cambridge. The coming of 'Advanced Level' changed all that. In 1958 the science department and in 1959 all departments entered second year specialists for 'A' level. But the shape of the curriculum and time-table meant that few boys could take more than two subjects. Up till 1964 less than fifty per cent of those leaving had two passes to their credit. Moreover the grades were not good enough. Statistically this looked serious, but it must be remembered that in those days Eton was resisting the national trend towards too early specialization and the cult of 'A' level as an end in itself. In 1964 the Head Master established a curriculum committee to look into the whole question and see whether two apparently incompatible aims could be reconciled. His brief emphasized three requirements: to provide thorough 'A' level preparation in three subjects for all boys so that they would leave with optimum academic qualifications, to spread the pressure of work more evenly over the five years of an Eton life, to keep a boy's general education on a broad basis for as long as possible and so delay the choice between Science and the Humanities, at that time a crucial one.

The committee's deliberations during the early part of 1965 showed that these aims involved painful clashes of interest. Each department was bidding for more teaching time and the classical subjects found themselves being squeezed out by modern ones. Inevitably, in the search for more time, covetous eyes were cast on the cherished Eton institutions of Pupil

Room* and Private Business.† Masters rallied eloquently to their support, none more eloquently than the Head of the History Department. 'Private Business makes education by discussion possible in a way which is impracticable in the school-room. It provides an unique opportunity to approach subjects not necessarily included in the syllabus in a way which can be chosen to suit the composition of a small group and its prevailing mood. It provides education in the fullest sense at a time when education is coming to involve simply the acquisition of superficial erudition in a narrow academic field. It provides the opportunity of an intimate professional relationship with boys over the whole of their specialist career . . . for a kind of teaching not possible in the division room, cultural in the strict sense of the term because free from concern with utility.' It would have been a pity if Eton had discarded an essential feature of its system just when schools elsewhere were striving to introduce small tutorial groups on the same pattern. In the summer of 1965 the committee presented its report and in June of that year the Head Master announced the new arrangements. The principal provisions were:

(i) That boys would take 'O' level in French, Latin, Elementary Maths and English Language at the end of their year in 'E' (usually the second).

(ii) That a diversified choice of courses would be offered for the year in 'D' (the third), leading towards but not determining the choice of specialization.

(iii) That the hours of work for specialists/sixth formers would be divided into four blocks of seven periods, code-named W X Y Z. In W, X and Y three subjects could be studied up to 'A' level.

To accommodate these proposals the number of school periods was raised from twenty-three to twenty-eight. The time 'after twelve', which up till 1964 gave an hour and a quarter of free time to some specialists, disappeared. Instead, many boys now had reading schools in their rooms, but at staggered times. Periods were set aside for Private Business and that other inestimable feature of the Eton programme, Extra Studies. This permitted boys to study a wide range of minority subjects on a non-departmental basis. In 1969 the following were offered: Russian, Swedish, German, Italian, English, Economics, Art, Mathematics, Social Studies, History of Art, Drama, The Business World, Music, Architecture, Archaeology, Philosophy, Africa, Machine Shop, Woodwork, Christian and Contemporary Problems.

* A period when the youngest boys are supervised by their classical tutors.

† Tutorials devoted to academic, cultural, sociological, etc., interests.

The new curriculum was much less rigid than the old grammar school programme. To some extent the third year, in 'D', could be adapted to a boy's individual preference. The new specialist found two hundred and ninety possible combinations of *main* subjects open to him. Such versatility could not be attained without an increase in the teaching staff and in 1965 the Provost and College approved the appointment of a dozen assorted linguists, scientists and English teachers.

The new system has been in operation for close on five years at the time of writing. Some of its consequences are worth noting. Every boy now has at least three encounters with the G.C.E. examining board and this has the effect of making him get into a higher gear earlier in his Eton career. Henceforth 'O', like 'A' level, will not be taken in December, for it was important not to have boys taking 'A' level after only five terms' preparation. Since our internal examination has been suppressed in the Lent half the Etonian of the future will probably take full-scale Trials only seven times in his career, as opposed to thirteen or more in the past. By contrast, every summer about 800 will be sitting G.C.E. This gearing up has meant that there are now far more specialists/sixth formers, 564 in 1969 and too many to fit into College Chapel. In one house of forty-nine, twenty-eight are specialists, mostly studying three main subjects.

G.C.E. qualifications are now of importance to a boy soon after he comes to the school. He needs a minimum of five 'O' levels to become a specialist. He knows that he must obtain 'A' levels to qualify him for the career of his choice, and needs top grades if he aspires to a university. All this has made Etonians much more conscious of the central importance of school work and constantly reminds them that they are in competition with the products of other schools of every kind. It has had one disquieting result. Clever boys are reaching 'A' level at an age when they are academically advanced but in other ways immature. But when they have taken this much-vaunted examination some of them naturally feel that there is nothing more for them to achieve at school and they leave early, missing some of the most formative experiences.

Growth and change in subjects   The subjects which have expanded most under the new curriculum are Geography, Economics and English.

GEOGRAPHY is an example of how vigorously a young plant can grow in ancient soil. After a tentative start at Eton, where it was introduced in 1954 to provide fodder for less able specialists, it was in 1965 established as a subject in its own right and soon won for itself the status of a serious academic discipline. The break-through came when it was accepted as part of the programme in 'D'. This provided the geographer specialist with an 'O' level background; though one candidate had already won an open award to Oxford on seven terms' work. In December 1967 fifty-five candidates took 'O' level after one year's preparation. Half of these boys chose Geography as one of their 'A' level subjects. In 1969 we find one hundred and four boys studying the subject for 'O' level and eighty doing the challenging new 'A' level courses. Geography attracts them partly because of its practical element and obvious relevance to modern life but also because it occupies a unique position between the natural sciences and the humanities. The teaching staff consists of three qualified geographers and two helpers. The departmental nerve-centre is at the southern corner of Cannon Yard. There are housed the Geography library of some eight hundred books and a 'book pound' of two thousand volumes. Equipment includes a complete set of one-inch Ordnance Survey maps covering the whole of Great Britain plus multiple sets for areas of particular geographical interest and a world coverage of roll maps. Special shelving and drawers accommodate photo transparencies, film strips, map extracts, information sheets and so on. As aids to teaching there are a 16 mm. film projector, an overhead projector, a photo-copier, a slide projector, and a complete set of survey equipment from a theodolite downwards. The West Tower, known to earlier generations as a smokers' den, now houses a reading-room and above is a meteorological station, inevitably dubbed the Air Ministry Roof. It boasts a Stevenson's screen together with a complete set of equipment—rain gauge, maximum and minimum temperature, a wet and dry bulb, a thermograph and an anemometer or wind-gauge. During the summer field expeditions take boys out into interesting country and for the future holiday schemes are envisaged at such places as the Durham University field centre. The department has excellent relations with universities which recognize Geography as a serious subject and know that it is taught to high standards at Eton. There is plenty of stimulus to read Geography as an honours course; the graduate can regard himself as well equipped for a career in commerce and industry, in the planning departments of the public service and in teaching.

ECONOMICS is another subject whose rapid growth in recent years may be attributed to its apparent practical advantages in a commercially minded society. It was, in fact, taught in Extra Studies a hundred years ago by William Johnson (afterwards Cory), composer of the Eton Boating Song. In our own time the Extra Studies division was started in 1957, and in 1959 the first candidates, taught by a mathematician and entirely without textbooks, passed 'A' level. Others were encouraged to follow and from 1959 to 1964 a considerable number of 'A' levels were obtained by candidates for whom this was a minority subject. Then at one and the same time the examining board's standard was raised and the subject was given full status in the 1965 curriculum reform. Boys of better calibre took up the subject, realizing that it is an intellectual discipline in which logical qualities are just as important as mathematical. By 1968 the numbers had risen from about twenty to one hundred and fifty, all of them specialists. In 1969 two hundred specialists were doing Economics, of whom half were taking 'A' level in July. The teaching staff consists of one master with an economics degree, two or three who have worked it up as an extra subject, and four borrowed from the History or Maths department. Until recently many candidates did four schools a week and some took the exam after one year. Competing against schools that allocated seven periods a week for two years, about seventy-five per cent of Etonians scored passes at 'A' level. In the last two years our economists have won four university awards and in several other awards there was an element of Economics. Out of seven who tried in 1967 two won awards.

ENGLISH can hardly be called a new subject at a school which nurtured Gray, Walpole, Shelley and Orwell, to name but a few. Yet ten years ago a master with a degree in English could not have that fact printed in the Eton Calendar. There was no such department. Of course it was taught, but it was taught by the old style of form master, or to give him his Eton title, the classical division master. But since 1965 English has been recognized as a subject, it has a place in the curriculum and appears after the names of no less than six masters in the staff list. Now two hundred and five specialists are studying it as a main subject and one hundred and sixty-three are doing it in their 'O' level year. In 1968 two awards were won at Oxford and Cambridge.

The older subjects have certainly not remained static in the midst of so much change. CLASSICS are now taught with a greater use of visual aids and the restored pronunciation, familiar to Erasmus, makes Latin sound more like a foreign language. Two language laboratories have given an electric boost to the teaching of MODERN LANGUAGES and new methods of rapid learning have produced excellent results in German, Russian, Spanish and Italian. The new MATHEMATICS has not touched Eton, but the Schools' Mathematical Project is teaching boys to apply theory to practical problems much earlier. HISTORY has not changed since the war; there is simply more of it. For the historian more than anyone else a vast supply of books is essential. The History Pound is an example of the kind of amenities that are now available to the Eton specialist. There are of course the School Library and the Henry Marten History Library (other libraries serve other subjects) but the History Pound meets the needs of the most voracious reader. For a fee of £2 per term specialists can borrow as many books as they like during the holidays as well as during schooltime. Close on fourteen thousand titles are available and their combined value is over £16,000. It is common for a boy to have £20 worth of books on loan at a time. The administration of this vast lending service is undertaken by a master in this department. Since 1964 the study of this subject has secured sixteen awards for Etonians at Oxford and Cambridge.

In no department however has the introduction of new equipment and methods been more meaningful than in SCIENCE. It is not generally appreciated what a strong science tradition Eton has. In 1903, under Dr. Porter, physics teachers were demonstrating the new discovery, radioactivity. Within a few years of Marconi's invention of wireless telegraphy transmissions were being conducted between Eton and Teddington. Such famous scientists as Alfred Egerton, Sir Thomas Merton, J. B. S. Haldane and T. E. Huxley were at Eton. In 1912 Whitelaw-Gray was conducting experiments on the rare gases and by 1914 H. G. Moseley had given the world the theory of atomic numbers. Two hundred years ago Eton was subscribing for copies of the *Philosophical Transactions* of the Royal Society.

The resurgence of Science began in the mid-fifties at just about the time when the Industrial Fund made their grant and the rebuilding of the Science Schools began. In 1955 about fourteen per cent of Eton specialists chose Maths and Science; now the number remains steady at about thirty per cent. The teaching staff has grown from eleven in 1955 to eighteen in 1969. Now, with its new buildings and equipment, the department is a thriving one. The laboratories offer facilities comparable to those available to a first year undergraduate course at a university. Three highly qualified laboratory technicians plus three assistants are available to set up perhaps two hundred different demonstrations a week. This increases the capacity of the teaching staff, who are free to prepare lessons, to teach or to give individual tuition. The Egerton room, aesthetically panelled and lavishly equipped, has closed-circuit television for making experiments visible to larger numbers or for telerecording and relaying TV educational broadcasts. The standard of Science at Eton is now on a par with the best schools in the country; fifteen awards have been won at Oxford and Cambridge in the last five years and later results show that our candidates do well at the university and thereafter. The myth that the science graduate is doomed to a life of research in the laboratory has long been exploded. Today scientists and engineers are occupying more and more key places in management, and the proportion will grow as industry becomes more specialised.

The SCIENCE syllabus has been changing with bewildering rapidity during the past decade and the pace shows no signs of slackening. It is becoming even more difficult for a non-scientist to comprehend what his colleagues in the laboratories are doing. Eton has however kept abreast of changes both as regards scientific apparatus and teaching methods, as a few examples of the equipment used and the topics included will show.

In CHEMISTRY use is made of ultra-violet and infra-red spectroscopy, and of vapour-phased chromatography for separating and identifying volatile organic liquids.

The PHYSICS department have recently acquired a helium-neon laser for optical experiments and demonstrations; they have counters and ratemeters for experiments in radioactivity and oscilloscopes and signal generators on a scale adequate for class use at specialist level. They are able to carry out a comprehensive range of electronic experiments in their laboratories.

For BIOLOGY there is available a wide range of micro-ecological set-ups, and strains of small animals are maintained for work on genetics. There is a comprehensive collection of colour transparencies as well as a good stock of microscopes and other conventional equipment.

If the pursuits of the more sophisticated scientists baffle the layman the biological problems exercising the minds of lower boys may bring some reassurance:

'How does a snail locomote? Using a lens observe the foot of a snail moving along the underside of a glass plate held horizontally in a retort stand. . . .

'Return the mouse to the litter. Handle it only by the tip of the tail or the scent of your fingers may well cause the mother to reject it.'

This brief survey of some of the changes in teaching inevitably omits much. To include the most significant feature is impossible: the good teacher has an individual freshness of approach, a gift for interpreting his own subject, which no one else is in a position to observe, much less describe.

10 · An index of change

There have been so many innovations at Eton that it is difficult to decide which to include and in what order. The list can be limited by linking something that has changed in the last twenty-five years with each letter of the alphabet. What follows is therefore a brief Index of major and minor innovations:

Americans It is becoming common for boys from the United States, and indeed from South Africa as well, to spend a term or a year at Eton after they have completed their schooling at home. There are also exchange schemes which bring German and Spanish boys to Eton in their final year.

Beating Beating as a means of punishment by senior boys has become a rarity and in some houses disappeared altogether. This is one symptom of a wider change of attitude; senior boys do not like to adopt authoritarian attitudes towards the younger ones. There is much more informality between the age-groups. Fagging continues on a much more humanized basis.

Combined Cadet Force The Eton C.C.F. has been a pioneer of change. The first big step was to make entry selective, based on house master's reports and an interview. There is room in the Corps for about half the specialists. Eton started the 'Greenfields Scheme', which permits schools to select their own annual camp sites—in our case Wales, Scotland and Norway. The courses offered to cadets are varied, interesting and sometimes challenging. This year thirty-two cadets applied to do parachuting, under the auspices of the Green Jackets Parachute Club, near Colchester.

Dress Dress remains unchanged where school uniform is concerned, except that braces are anathema to modern boys. But they no longer wear it when they have leave away from Eton. Within certain fairly liberal rules Etonians in 'change' have much more freedom. But the tweed jacket and collar and tie are still favoured by the school authorities.

Entry Entry is still on the house basis. Moves to reform our system usually founder on the fact that there is likely to be a lapse of thirteen years between decision and result. Entry has been made easier for some since boys who have not had the opportunity of learning Latin need not take it in Common Entrance. In cases of financial difficulty help from the War Memorial Fund is available to all Etonians and from the Camrose Bursaries for any deserving candidate for entry. These funds have been in operation since respectively 1944 and 1952.

Festivals   Festivals have in many cases had to yield to practical considerations. The Fourth of June now occurs on the nearest Saturday and even then is less enthusiastically supported, perhaps because the evening fireworks have been discontinued. The Lords match is now played after the half has ended, and attendance is falling away.

Games   There is less support for organized team games nowadays and more enthusiasm for an individual game like squash. Senior boys are tending to opt out of cricket and rowing in favour of a more diversified fare of tennis, golf, sailing and so on. The field game survives in the Michaelmas half and in the Lent soccer has gained at the expense of rugger, probably because it is played on a house basis.

Hair   Hair, following the national trend, has become longer and longer. It looks terrible with school uniform and arouses much adverse comment, but it is not a reliable guide to moral standards.

Idleness   'Idleness', Robert Burton noted, 'is an appendix to nobility'. Today's noble young are aware that society does not consider it owes them a living and are not noticeably more prone to idleness than their fellows; the programme of close on six hundred sixth-formers includes three 'A' level subjects.

Jobs   Jobs which Etonians take up when they leave have not changed greatly. Data have been made available on 150 of those who left in 1963 and whose careers are known. The number going into the armed forces has dropped sharply;

AN INDEX OF CHANGE

agriculture and engineering have on the contrary attracted increased numbers.
The top ten careers for this vintage of Etonians are: armed forces (23),
banking and Stock Exchange (22), commerce and industry (18), accountancy
(13), estate and land agency (12), law (12), teaching (8), journalism (6),
agriculture (5) and engineering (5). Etonians are still scarce in medicine (2) and
the Church (1) but the returns show one ballet dancer, one hotel manager and
three social workers. The Careers room, run by a member of the modern
language staff, is hard by the 'Pop' room. It is an efficient-looking executive
office equipped with the very comprehensive card index and file system of
C.R.A.C. (Careers Research and Advisory Centre) which is in fact run by an
Old Etonian. The increasing number of boys who come for careers advice find
plenty of display material and literature and can be quickly put in touch with
individual firms or professional bodies. A significant pointer has been the interest
shown in the two 'Challenge of Industry' Conferences which have been held
here, organized by the Industrial Society. For two days all other work stopped
so that senior boys could attend lectures in the new theatre and then discuss
problems in small groups with the thirty visitors who came.

King's　King's scholars may henceforth come from a wider sector, since the entrance
Scholars　examination for College was altered. Ten papers used to be compulsory:
　　　　　Maths (2), Latin (3), Latin and Greek Grammar, Greek, English Essay, General
　　　　　Paper, French. Of these only Maths, English Essay and the General Paper are
　　　　　compulsory. Of the rest candidates must take four or five. There has so far
　　　　　been practically no response from candidates in the public sector to this offer
　　　　　of a first-class education at minimal cost.

Limits　The old 'five mile limit' went long ago. There is no distance limit, and senior
　　　　　boys are allowed much greater freedom of movement, though trips to London
　　　　　are more rigidly controlled.

Music　Music has had a renaissance and in addition to the Eton College Musical
　　　　　Society and the school orchestra there are now the second orchestra, the brass
　　　　　ensemble, the music circle, the madrigal society and the corps band. Instead

of the Choir School the Foundation will now be awarding three music scholarships a year to oppidan houses. When they reach their total of fifteen these scholars should make a very big impact on the musical standards of the whole school.

Noise Noise is now an acute problem, for the increasing traffic from London Airport is often directed straight over Eton. Masters continually have to break off teaching while the passing jets squirt ulcerated executives to business conferences across the Atlantic.

Old boys Old boys support Old Boy Day less and less. In some houses football teams are still raised but in most the day is meaningless if not embarrassing. It seems that this kind of association with the place of education is a thing of the past. Old boys prefer to return individually and make more personal contacts.

Permissive-ness Permissiveness pervades every aspect of society today. The unbridled permissiveness of the society outside inevitably seeps through the metaphorical walls of Eton. The task of the house master is to find a sensible balance between too rigorous authoritarianism and galloping anarchy, and every day this balance becomes more delicate.

Quotation 'Our age is an age of scepticism, every one of our institutions is on trial. Each must be dug up by the roots by our political and social gardeners, and its growth and health criticised, examined and searched with microscopic exactitude.' (Wasey Sterry, *Annals of Eton*, 1898.) *Plus ça change* . . .

Religion Religion is, as it always has been and always must be, a burning question. The Statutes of Eton make it clear that this is a predominantly religious foundation. That is why the Chapel remains the central feature of the place, and boys must attend daily services. Among a number of changes under this heading the most easily identified are the reduction of compulsory services on Sunday to one, a greater variety in the forms of service, the reading of week-day lessons by boys, the increased pastoral role of the chaplains. Full treatment of the question of religion in the school would require a whole volume.

Social service Social service is perhaps the most significant innovation in recent times. It has involved Etonians with the problems of this very problematical neighbourhood, though many of the people served do not know where their young helpers come from. The number of volunteers is at present ninety-five. There is no pressure on them to volunteer and they do the work in their own free time. Some of the tasks they undertake are particularly demanding; they pay visits to families whose problems defy description, teach elementary English to Indian and Pakistani children to enable them to understand the teachers when they go to school, entertain mentally handicapped people of all ages at the Slough Friendly Club and give help to those who have never learned to read or write at the Remedial Reading Class. The other activities—hospitals, nurseries, visits to the blind—are more conventional youth service activities. All are challenging assignments and the impact of these experiences on young minds needs careful watching. Therefore the work is followed up by seminars and discussions guided by a doctor specializing in mental problems. All this widens boys' horizons by giving them first-hand experience of the social problems of the day and at the same time a chance to do something positive about them on the most meaningful level—the personal one. Now many individuals and communities in the area really have something to be grateful to Eton for.

Teachers Teachers have increased in number by thirty per cent over twenty-five years. Whereas in the past almost half of them were Etonians now only two in the junior half of the staff were at school here. This is not due to any official policy but to a change of attitude amongst Old Etonians. The attitude of boys towards beaks is now a good deal more informal and relaxed, perhaps because they come together for more activities such as societies, acting, expeditions. The teaching staff is subject to more frequent changes because many younger masters stay at Eton for only a few years.

University University in the old days used to mean Oxford or Cambridge. That situation has now changed. The State has subsidized a vast expansion of universities, and at the same time provided the means for those with good enough qualifications to attend. Britain's university system is the most democratic, for the percentage of students who are sons of manual workers is higher than in any other country in the western world. The present student population of 380,000 may well double in the next twelve years. Amidst all this Etonians find the competition much keener. The result is that although as many Etonians as before go to university they go to a wider range of universities. Paradoxically the number of awards to Oxford and Cambridge has gone up. This table shows numbers gaining university places in the last five years:

Year of Entry	CambrOx	Others in G.B.	Total	CambrOx Awards
1965	67	23	90	22
1966	67	32	99	19
1967	72	34	106	16
1968	73	38	111	25
1969	82	not available		19

As can be seen 1968 was a high point. In that year one house gained ten places at CambrOx, another gained four awards and the pupils of one modern tutor won three awards.

In recent years a master has taken on the special task of maintaining contact with all universities—he has personally visited twenty-seven of them—advising boys and their tutors on the choice and helping in the complex business of entry. Only lately have proper records been kept and figures published. They show that for 1969 133 boys put CambrOx as their first choice and twenty-five put some other university. Altogether fifty universities figure on the applications; the most popular after CambrOx were Bristol, Edinburgh, Durham, Exeter, Kent, York and Sussex. Whilst the boys have accepted this trend it is still hard to persuade parents that the situation is not what it was 'in my day'. A sign of the times was the dinner given in College Hall in Michaelmas 1968, when about fifty dons, lecturers, wardens and professors from universities all over Britain came to Eton as guests of the College. They spent a night in boys' houses and next day had a chance to see what a modern Eton education means. Nothing could have indicated more clearly that the days of reliance on a few familiar colleges at Oxford and Cambridge are

over and that Eton desires to strengthen its links with the new seats of higher
education.

V.S.O. Voluntary Service Overseas has taken many leavers to lonely and demanding
tasks in distant lands. Others have volunteered to work for Bridge in Britain, at
a Kibbutz or some other organization to help the under-privileged. A great
many Etonians, when they leave school, seek some experience that will form a
complete contrast to their past or future lives.

Windsor Windsor is out of bounds up till boys' dinner on working days. The area
north-east of a line Thames Street, Peascod Street is permanently forbidden, as
is the town of Slough. The housing and industrial developments in this district
and the new populations they have attracted have drastically altered Eton's
immediate environment.

X-days X-Days or holidays are now completely clear of schools and private business as
well as of organized games; this leaves the day free for expeditions. Such days
are now spaced out on a more rational basis and not fixed to the festivals of red-
letter saints. Lady Day, because of its association with the Founder's devotion,
remains a sacrosanct holiday at the very end of the Lent half.

Year The arrangement of the school year has been much affected by the dates fixed
by the Joint Board for that external examination, the General Certificate of
Education. G.C.E. now begins well before the end of June. This imposes an
earlier start to the summer holidays and a very long Michaelmas schooltime.
The tradition of beginning and ending on a Wednesday has had to go by the
board and the future of Long Leave is uncertain.

Zion Zion, we know, is the City of God. One thing at Eton has not changed. On the
last day of every half 'Jerusalem' is still sung in College Chapel. But how, in
1970, does one build Jerusalem in England's green and pleasant land? Wasey

AN INDEX OF CHANGE

Sterry's statement of the purpose of an Eton education, 'to teach the higher patriotism', is too abstract for today, yet the attempt to define it more clearly must necessarily be of a personal nature.

The spectacle of our present world, 'multitudes, multitudes in the valley of decision', must convince the reflective observer that mankind will destroy itself unless leaders of sufficient stature emerge to control the wavering herds. Somewhere must be nurtured the thinkers who will take the frontiers of knowledge forward on their next great advance. We saw the renaissance of the humanities in the fifteenth century, the industrial revolution in the nineteenth. In our own century we have seen the explosion of scientific knowledge; we have lived with the hydrogen bomb for two decades only to learn that we are now sitting on a biological time bomb. The next phase, if we are to survive as recognizable humans, must be a redressing of the balance. That can only be achieved by men of extraordinary ability, whose specialized knowledge is seated on as broad a base as possible, whose horizons have been kept constantly wide, whose knowledge of science does not blind them to the message of the humanities, whose powers of self-expression have not been sacrificed to the acquisition of data, who can, finally, place scientific advance in its proper relation to history, human psychology and ethical truth.

Appendix

A list in alphabetical order of boys' houses at present in use with a note on

date of construction,
licensed numbers (indicated in brackets),
the origin of the name of the house,
architectural features of particular interest,
improvements carried out 1950–70,
holders of the house during the present century, with the date of their
entry.

Note: Houses at Eton are known generally by the name of the house master rather than by the name of the building. House masters usually move house once during their time, when a preferable house becomes vacant, and all the boys go too. That is why the same name appears under several houses. The reason why some houses have had more occupants is that people are usually anxious to get out of them fast. For instance Carter House is not only decrepit but stands on the High Street. Masters whose names appear in brackets are those unfortunates who, for the convenience of the College or a senior colleague, had to squat in a vacated house for one Half.

Angelo's Late eighteenth century. (42)
Miss Sophia Angelo, 'the duchess of Eton', lived here. Doorway with wood panelled pilasters, 'Tower of the Wind' capitals, entablature with medallion cornice, traceried fanlight. (Scheduled Grade 2 by Ministry.) Due for extension and improvement.

R. S. Kindersley	1903	A. C. Sheepshanks	1925	P. S. H. Lawrence	1951
M. D. Hill	1908	C. J. Rowlatt	1930	G. R. St. Aubyn	1960
C. H. Blakiston	1921	R. J. N. Parr	1945	(Hon.)	

Baldwin's Bec 1862 and 1964. (48)
The name goes back to pre-Foundation times. See pp. 51–53.

H. E. Luxmoore	1872–1902	J. F. Crace	1923	G. I. Brown	1956
H. T. Bowlby (Rev.)	1902	H. H.-S. Hartley	1935	B. J. W. Hill	1964
E. W. Stone	1909	W. W. Williams	1951		

Carter Eighteenth century. (42)
Thomas Carter was Usher 1705–16. Later members of the family were and are prominent in Eton's affairs. Roman Doric doorway with three-quarter columns on plinths and traceried fanlights; original wrought-iron railings. (Scheduled Grade 3.) Not improved. May cease to be a boys' house.

R. S. de Havilland	1901	W. G. Tatham	1934	R. D. F. Wild (Rev.)	1951
C. M. Wells	1905	J. M. Peterson	1938	D. H. Macindoe	1956
F. W. Dobbs	1917	N. G. Wykes	1944	M. A. Nicholson	1962
A. C. Sheepshanks	1922	T. A. Brocklebank	1946	M. D. Neal	1963
A. H. G. Kerry	1925	W. W. Williams	1949	R. J. G. Payne	1967
C. E. Sladden	1929				

Common Lane Early eighteenth century. (40)
Sited at the head of Common Lane. Six-panel door with fine traceried fanlight; old tiled roof with hipped gables to the side elevation. (Scheduled Grade 3.) Not yet improved.

H. Brinton	1900	L. Todd	1916	M. N. Forrest	1955
E. W. Stone	1904	W. Hope-Jones	1924	B. Rees	1963
S. G. Lubbock	1909	G. W. Nickson	1939	C. A. Impey	1965

Cotton Hall 1869–70. (48)
Takes the ancient name of this part of the manor of Eton. Major improvements 1968. Private side extended, a better house master's study created; kitchen modernized, new space built for staff accommodation and boys' wash rooms; space made for three extra boys' rooms; central heating.

E. Impey	1899–1907	G. J. Chitty (Rev.)	1925	C. D'O. Gowan	1947
R. P. L. Booker	1907	C. Mayes	1931	J. Anderson	1964
A. W. Whitworth	1920				

Durnford 1845. (48)
Its first occupant was Rev. F. E. ('Judy') Durnford, who also gave his name to

'Judy's Passage'. Neo-Tudor style. New kitchen 1954; major improvements and extension 1964. See pp. 64–65.

M. D. Hill	1907	J. D. Upcott	1927	A. J. Marsden	1952
H. de Havilland	1908	W. N. Roe	1934	P. Hazell	1957
A. E. Conybeare	1910	H. Babington-		R. D. Macnaghten	1964
J. C. Chute (Rev.)	1921	Smith	1937		

Evans's (45)

Bought, restored and extended by William Evans in 1837 and thereafter associated with that family until 1906. Miss Evans was the last of the Dames who held houses.

A. B. Ramsey	1906	R. C. Martineau	1944	D. H. Macindoe	1962
J. C. Butterwick	1926				

Farrer 1959. (49)

Named after Gaspard Farrer. See pp. 59–60.

F. J. R. Coleridge	1959	J. D. R. McConnell	1966

Godolphin *Circa* 1722. (46)

Named after Provost Godolphin (1695–1733). One of the first to be built as a boys' house and one of the first to be modernized. Late eighteenth-century porch in the Adam manner with traceried fanlight and flanking columns, which are continued in the hall; interesting bow windows at rear. (Scheduled Grade 2.) Major restoration and extension 1955: wash rooms, improved staff accommodation, room for five more boys; central heating.

A. M. Goodhart	1905	H. K. Marsden	1930	F. W. How	1946
T. F. Cattley	1914	J. H. L. Lambart	1933	(J. Anderson	1964)
				P. Hazell	1964

Hawtrey 1845. (42)

Rev. J. W. Hawtrey was the first occupant. Neo-Tudor and a twin of Durnford

House. An example of Victorian stone and brickwork and pointing. Not yet improved.

R. P. L. Booker	1901	J. H. L. Lambart	1928	K. R. Spencer	1963
C. H. K. Martin	1907	J. D. Hills	1933	C. W. Willink	1964
G. J. Chitty (Rev.)	1918	A. K. Wickham	1935	D. N. Callender	1968
R. A. Young	1925	F. J. A. Cruso	1946		

Hodgson 1842. (say 46)

Provost Hodgson was the builder of New Buildings. Known as 'the gin palace' when first built because of its luxury. Now used for decanting. Its future is undecided. On this site was proposed the multi-storey boys' house that never was.

R. S. Kindersley	1901	A. C. Beasley-		D. P. Simpson	1956
L. S. R. Byrne	1902	Robinson	1930	R. H. Parry	1962
A. C. Rayner-Wood	1912	W. R. Colquhoun	1937	Music Schools	1966
G. W. Headlam	1920	W. M. M. Milligan	1946	'College'	1967
E. W. Powell	1925	D. G. Bousfield	1950	O. R. S. Bull	1968

Holland *Circa* 1800. (45)

Major restoration and extension have been carried out in three distinct phases: new boys' wing pushed out 1955, allowing room for wash rooms, staff accommodation and increased capacity. Central heating; new main kitchen summer holidays 1965. New pantry and private side kitchenette, etc., in 1968–9.

R. C. Radcliffe (Rev.)	1898	A. C. Sheepshanks	1930	N. G. Wykes	1946
J. H. M. Hare	1907	W. G. Tatham	1938	P. S. H. Lawrence	1960
A. E. Conybeare	1921	O. Van Oss	1940	C. W. Willink	1968

Hopgarden 1825. (46)

On this site were grown hops for College audit ale. Major improvements in 1968–9: new boys' staircase and staff accommodation, new Dame's suite, four new boys' rooms, rewired, private side improved, central heating.

T. C. Porter (Rev.)	1901	J. D. Hills	1935	M. D. Neal	1967
E. L. Churchill	1904	J. S. Herbert	1940	T. S. B. Card	1969
G. W. Headlam	1925	D. G. Bousfield	1955		

Jourdelay's 1720. (47)
The Founder originally acquired the site from one named Jourdelay. Hipped Welsh slate roof. (Scheduled Grade 2.) New kitchen. Central heating station built in garden, blending with surroundings.

H. C. Macnaghten	1899	H. E. E. Howson	1931	T. A. Brocklebank	1946
A. C. Rayner-Wood	1920	C. R. N. Routh	1933	O. Van Oss	1946
F. W. Dobbs	1922	R. T. Assheton	1934	D. P. Simpson	1962

Keate 1788. (42)
The famous Dr. Keate lived here 1809 to 1834. Built by Dr. Goodall. Pedimented doorway with Roman Doric pilasters on plinths; all tile hipped roof; original cast-iron railings. Due for decanting and major restoration 1970.

P. Williams	1901	H. M. McNeile	1919	(M. A. Nicholson	1961)
A. R. Somerville	1904	J. D. Upcott	1933	S. J. McWatters	1961
R. S. de Havilland	1908	D. C. Wilkinson	1945	M. A. Nicholson	1963

Manor (43)
On this site was the residence of the Lord of the Manor. Much rebuilt in nineteenth century. Major restoration begun 1969.

H. Broadbent	1899–1914	A. H. G. Kerry	1929	G. I. Brown	1963
V. le Neve Foster	1914	E. P. Hedley	1946	K. R. Spencer	1964
S. G. Lubbock	1916				

Mustians 1938. (50)
Named after a much older house on this site. The only boys' house built between

the two world wars. In 1965 an extension was built over the kitchen with new staff rooms, which freed former staff rooms for boys' modern wash-rooms; central heating. In summer 1966 fire destroyed about ten rooms and the roof, which was replaced without the now redundant chimneys but with partitions to break fire.

A. C. Beasley-Robinson	1937	R. J. N. Parr	1951	(R. D. Macnaghten	1966)
A. K. Wickham	1946	A. J. Marsden	1962	R. D. Baird	1966

Penn 1860. (49)

John Penn, whose arms are now placed on a front wall, was Lord of the Manor. 'A High Victorian white brick horror' (Pevsner). 'Yellow brown stocks' (Hussey). Major improvements and extension 1967 while house was occupied: pleasantly gabled new wing at back to provide more boys' rooms; a new Library and staff accommodation; new staircase to all floors; wash rooms and showers; new kitchen and pantry; private side extended with garden room, bedroom suite and kitchen; sills of boys' rooms lowered; redecorated throughout; central heating; garden replanned.

F. C. Austen Leigh	1869–1904	F. E. Robeson	1912	J. D. R. McConnell	1959
P. Williams	1904	C. A. Gladstone	1925	A. G. Ray	1966
		H. K. Prescot (Dr.)	1943		

South Lawn 1904. (49)

A house of this name, built in 1869, was extended in 1904. Major improvements 1966–7 while the house was occupied: three new wash rooms each with two baths, three showers and basins; extended 'rears'; Library bathroom; dining room enlarged; pupil room created; improved staff accommodation; reorganized kitchen and scullery; new garage and store space; rewired and replumbed; central heating.

H. F. W. Tatham	1905	M. D. Hill	1921	F. J. R. Coleridge	1949
A. E. Conybeare	1909	J. C. Chute (Rev.)	1927	B. J. W. Hill	1959
R. S. de Havilland	1910	W. N. Roe	1937	F. P. E. Gardner	1964

Timbralls 1823. (47)

The name dates from the original construction of Eton, when the near-by field was used as a depot for timber. It may at one time have been called 'Timberhaw'. Partially improved 1956–7: extension to westward with three new boys' rooms, bath and wash rooms; new Dame's accommodation replaced the back stairs; boys' entrance moved from Slough Road to New Schools Yard.

F. H. Rawlins	1900	L. S. Fortescue	1933	P. S. H. Lawrence	1959
R. S. Kindersley	1908	C. R. N. Routh	1934	R. M. A. Bourne	1960
E. W. Slater	1920	T. A. Brocklebank	1949		

Villiers 1962. (49)

Named after Arthur Villiers. See pp. 60–61.

D. J. Graham-Campbell	1962	(C. W. Willink	1964)	G. I. Brown	1965

Walpole 1907. (49)

Robert Walpole was the first 'Colleger' Prime Minister. (Harold Macmillan was the second.) Neo-Georgian. Major improvement 1965–6 while house was occupied: new and better wash rooms, bathrooms and 'rears'; improved staff accommodation (e.g. three-room suite for cook, bathrooms for boys' maids); new kitchen; three extra boys' rooms; private side kitchenette; central heating.

E. Impey	1907	A. W. Whitworth	1925	P. S. Snow	1946
T. F. Cattley	1914	H. K. Marsden	1933	M. N. Forrest	1963
A. M. Goodhart	1914				

Warre 1860. (43)

Edmund Warre occupied this house from 1869 until he became Head Master in 1884. It was built by Canon Hawtrey for his son immediately after Penn House and in much the same style. It was intended more as a private school than as a boys' house. Not yet improved.

S. A. Donaldson (Rev.)	1894	G. W. Lyttelton (Hon.)	1925	A. J. Marsden	1957
H. Brinton	1904	G. A. D. Tait	1944	C. N. C. Addison	1962

Waynflete 1901. (49)

Waynflete was the second Provost (1442) and builder of the ante-chapel. Neo-Tudor. Decanted for major restoration and extension 1968–9: new wing at eastern end provides room for improved staff accommodation, new bathrooms, wash rooms and 'rears'; new Dame's suite, kitchen reorganized, etc.; pupil room recreated (it had been partitioned to form boys' rooms); private side kitchenette; central heating; redecorated throughout and new-style fitted furnishings installed in all boys' rooms.

| A. C. G. Heygate | 1905 | R. A. Young | 1928 | R. D. F. Wild | 1956 |
| C. H. K. Marten | 1918 | L. H. Jaques | 1940 | O. R. S. Bull | 1969 |

Westbury 1901. (48)

Westbury was the fourth Provost (1447). Neo-Tudor. Decanted for major restoration and extension 1966–7. Private side pushed out westwards, space over this and over boiler house used to provide extra accommodation; new staff wing with all mod. cons.; extra boys' rooms raised capacity by four; private side brought up to standard with new kitchenette and house master's study; redecorated throughout with new style furnishings in boys' rooms; central heating.

A. H. Allcock	1900	C. E. Sladden	1934	D. J. Graham-	
C. A. Somerville	1905	D. C. Wilkinson	1941	Campbell	1951
C. M. Wells	1917	W. R. Colquhoun	1944	R. D. Baird	1962
C. J. M. Adie	1926			R. H. Parry	1967

Wotton 1903. (48)

Wotton was a Provost of the early seventeenth century. Due for partial improvement.

E. L. Vaughan	1903	H. H.-S. Hartley	1933	(D. G. Bousfield	1950)
L. S. R. Byrne	1912	A. C. Huson	1934	W. M. M. Milligan	1950
L. Todd	1924	G. A. D. Tait	1941	C. E. D. Chamier	1954
E. W. Powell	1930	J. M. Peterson	1944	C. A. Impey	1969

Index

INDEX

570